QUEST
for 5000
Birds

By Jim Stevenson

VanJus Press
Galveston

Photographs
All photos by Jim Stevenson

Cover Design and Layout
Justine Gilcrease

ISBN 0-9666438-6-0
Library of Congress Cataloging-in-Publication
Data applied for

DEDICATION

To Jackson, Becca, Chris, Bethannie and all my
former students —

In case you ever wondered where Snakeman went
every summer.

TABLE OF CONTENTS

PREFACE

My absolutely earliest recollection in life was as a small boy in the mid-1950s, specifically an incident that is of no earthshaking import. My father, who was arguably the dean of Florida ornithologists as a professor at Florida State University, was heading out to Lake Jackson, just north of Tallahassee, to count birds. I began accompanying him on birding forays, as it had occurred to me early on that if I wanted to spend time with my father, I had to go bird watching.

So, "we" fastened the old aluminum Grumman canoe (which still sits in my front yard) on his classic VW bug, and off we went. My only real memory of this excursion's birds was watching a medium-sized dark bird fly right past me where I was sitting insecurely in the front of this smallish boat. To this day, nearly a half-century later, I distinctly remember dad saying, in that instructive voice, "adult Little Blue Heron," (I suppose my first life bird) and taking out his personalized field card to record the bird's occurrence.

That's what my dad did. He was into quantitative field analysis of Florida birds: their distribution, nesting grounds, seasonal trends, and population dynamics. There were few ornithologists in Florida at the time, and really not too many birders. That's an amazing thought! But dad was the authority, he wrote "the book," and that quest quite frankly took his life eventually.

To spend time with my dad was to be exposed to the outdoors, not just the birds, but their homes, and other kinds of creatures, too. My dad knew the plants well, armed with his degree in botany, but knew he was pushing the envelope trying to excite me over those green things which provided perches for birds. To this day, as thankful as I am for his early zoology tutelage, my fascination later in life for North Florida's climax and serial communities could have benefitted greatly from this untapped wisdom.

I may not have appreciated birds fully, as few kids do, but they were a useful tool for gaining my dad's approval. My identifying all but the rare birds on sight brought the attaboys I craved, but discerning the songs of Summer Tanagers, Blue Grosbeaks and Orchard Orioles at a great distance delighted him no end.

He had quite a bit less enthusiasm for my other big zoological interest, spawned nearly the same year as the Lake Jackson incident so long ago. We were walking the flood plain surrounding Lake Munson, at the time a cesspool south of Tallahassee, when I turned over a cypress log and stared for some time at a creature that captivated my attention in ways that birds at that time failed to do.

It was a snake, specifically a Banded Watersnake, a harmless species of southern swamps. I called my dad for an identification, and he provided me information with the same enthusiasm I identify starlings, House Sparrows and pigeons for my clients today. He did get some amusement from the results of my rudely picking this small reptile up from its hiding place, and suddenly finding its disproportionately large teeth imbedded in my right index finger. To my dying day I will remember him saying, "I said it was harmless; that means nonpoisonous. I never said it wouldn't bite."

This began a relationship with the villain of The Garden that occupies a special place in my head and heart, and seems to complement my love and study of their feathered cousins. Snakes are the hands-on part of my field work, the testosterone connection of my psyche, and the underdog that I pull for as the world seems to demand their execution. Birds and snakes. Snakes and birds. Together they make the outdoors a whole place for me.

Yes, this is a book about the desire to locate and identify birds, but you must forgive me when I diverge and share the excitement of a world full of all kinds of creatures: water buffalo, little green spiders, sharks, and yes, snakes. Moreover, if there is a snake that moves, it seems there is a need to catch it, hold it, feel it, let it crawl on me, and release it gently back into its haunt.

Still, with this almost childhood fascination with scaley creatures, birds are my life, professionally and personally, and seem to be the focus of my existence each day. Connecting people with birds, either through field trips or my writing, is an all-encompassing goal that consumes my days, and frankly, a fair portion of many nights. In some ways, it keeps my father alive.

So come with me as I take you through six continents, hair-raising close calls, near-death accidents, and many of the truly remarkable and rare birds of the world.

CHAPTER ONE

THE BUDDING BIRDER

My childhood was normal enough. I played baseball, wasn't overly fond of school, thought girls were creepy, and played football with the neighborhood guys. My secret life was birds, fostered by a father, Dr. Henry Stevenson, who was proud to have a son who knew birds pretty well. Saturday field trips gave me my dad all to myself, and they were generally fun, but always instructive under the professor.

Sundays were for church, followed by a large, southern-style family meal. Early on, this was with my three older siblings, and we ate like hounds. The sizable portion miraculously uneaten was the fare for weekday nights, when Mother couldn't possibly teach school and cook every night. After Sunday dinner, though, it was out to the boonies for me! There was a huge Beech/Magnolia forest on the other side of the railroad tracks fairly untouched and loaded with animals. Southern Dusky Salamanders,

Gray Rat Snakes, Flying Squirrels and Bronzed Frogs were but a few of nature's gifts in this unspoiled wilderness.

Walking into "my" forest during the breeding season was like being hit with a wall of sound. There were not just common species like cardinals, titmice and Blue Jays. Gracing this avian paradise were Hooded Warblers, Wood Thrushes, Yellow-throated Vireos, parulas and Acadian Flycatchers, to name a few. I would always carry my cheap 7 X 35 binoculars, but with my keen eyes and trained ears, I seldom used them. Mostly, they beat my face to a pulp when I took off after the speedy Black Racers that were so much fun to catch.

After school during the week, with an alternative of homework, I would forsake books for walks in this cool, moist jungle. Every day I had a new experience, ran across a new animal and learned new things. Moreover, I learned to get along with myself, and like who I was. I was at peace with the world, my identity, and God. I pretended some-

times in front of the neighborhood boys, but in my element I could love birds and chase snakes.

My dad was quite the taskmaster, making sure I progressed in my ability to identify birds. He didn't seem to care so much about other aspects of birds, and he developed a particular disdain for the budding science of ecology, especially as it related to ornithology. He was raised in the old school at Cornell, had many of the greats of yesteryear for professors (like Arthur Allen) and classmates (like Allen Phillips), and concentrated his efforts on issues of quantitative field distribution. This was the time he began trusting me enough to take data on my own for his research, which gave me great satisfaction and confidence.

These short trips were around rural parts of Tallahassee, for an hour or two in duration. It was amazing how he could take my field card and find any bird I wasn't positive of, and dismantle my rationale for its identification. How did he know that wasn't a Hairy Woodpecker? What told him it was too early for a White-throated Sparrow? I didn't know what he had, but I wanted it myself!

My dad may have been tough on me about birds, but I didn't feel like the Lone Ranger. He got so exasperated with some local birders, especially for some Christmas Bird Count records they tried to get past him, he resorted to giving bird skin tests. Sometimes, I can't believe he did that! There were all the usual excuses, like "this is so different from seeing the bird in the wild." But honestly, you wouldn't believe some of their misidentifications, and these by folks who regarded themselves as the last word on bird identification.

Growing up I may not have been the quickest, but there

◀ *Wood Thrush*

were two incidents involving these tests that will always make me proud (and smug). The first involved a huge bird skin test Dad inflicted on just about every birder in North Florida. There were all kinds of tough stuff there, including fall warblers, sparrows, peeps and female ducks. I mean, it was a bear.

We all went in with great fear and trepidation, but this one older lady saw me with pencil and paper (I was about ten years old) and said in a most patronizing voice, "Oh, Jimmy, it's so sweet that you're going to try a few birds." Grrrr! Not much bothered this fat little kid, but she really inspired me to do well. And apparently I did, for with the exception of Dad's two graduate students, John Ogden and Frank Chapman, I had the highest score. I'll give my dad credit for that

An even sweeter victory involved my eldest brother, Ernie. He has always been better than I at everything, a typical big/little brother story. He's smarter than I, more spiritual, is a better shot, has a lot more money, a beautiful wife, and is much more likable. If only he was funny.

Back then, we used to handle the boat party for the Christmas Bird Counts together. Ernie would drive the boat while I recorded birds, although he was no slouch at bird identification – especially the ducks he used to blow to Mars. We bounced along those wicked waves all day long when it was so cold, in his words, "you didn't care whether you lived or died."

Invariably, we'd wind up arguing about what some bird was, and my dad would have to sort it out. One day, he had enough, and laid out a slough of birds on the lab in 109 Conradi at FSU, for the skin test at the OK Corral. When the smoke cleared, it was nice to be better than he at something, and we never debated birds again. Like the earlier bird skin test, I'll give my dad the teacher, the credit.

Experiences like these may have been little pieces that led to who I am now, but the real moment that altered the direction of my life was a chance meeting with the ornithologist – Roger Tory Peterson. He came to Tallahassee for an Audubon lecture series, and my parents took him (and me) out to dinner. Dr. Peterson was really nice, and treated me like I was a real person. But during the course of our sharing, I remembered him mentioning that he had seen more than five thousand species of birds around the world. Five thousand! That's with three zeros. My life list at the time was 286. It is the oddest thing that I apparently misunderstood him, as he didn't actually see 5000 until later in his life. But the hook was set.

In that moment, I pledged to myself that I would one day see five thousand species of birds, but I had no idea what a life voyage that promise would take me on. Believe me, it was a long and winding road (especially those through the tropics).

As I became a teenager, I discovered another type of creature, the loveliest of them all: girls. Birds fell temporarily behind snakes, baseball and the fairer sex. I was also crazy enough to be in my school's band and chorus, as well as student government. I still birded some, but this hiatus proved useful, as one day the importance of our feathered friends finally came into sharp focus.

One incident shortly after high school very nearly ended my odyssey before it ever began. On an unusually warm evening, I took my high school sweetheart, Rachel, out "road cruising" for snakes, and nearly bought the farm. Road cruising is simply driving old country roads around dusk and picking up snakes crossing, or warming themselves on the asphalt.

On this particular night, we were really hauling them in. Of particular importance were two Mud Snakes, a nonaggressive species, with shiny red and black vertical markings and a black nose. Then there was another snake, and I clearly saw red and black. With Rachel's foot on the brake, I ran behind the car and grabbed the shiny snake before it could escape. Too bad it was a Coral Snake.

The serpent reached around like lightning and nailed me on my left pinky, causing me to realize it could not be the gentle Mud Snake. As my eyes adjusted, I saw the narrow yellow rings, almost obscured by the red brake lights, and knew I was in a heap of trouble. The size of the snake — nearly a yard long — also led me to think it couldn't have been the deadly but diminutive Coral Snake, but you know what they say about assumptions.

At any rate, I drove to the hospital as fast as I could, winding out that Nova at about warp nine. With the deadly neurotoxin creeping through my lymph vessels toward my spinal cord, there was very little the doctor could do, so he asked to call my pastor. I declined, and as my parents were out of town, it was a long, lonely night.

The acidic protein enzyme caused unbelievable hallucinations, with vivid colors and wild dreams. But amazingly, I dreamed of birds, and felt comfortable with whatever fate befell me. Nausea hit during the night as well, then some problems breathing. But it wasn't my time to die, and I was back at work running camps for kids, with one day's recuperation. My doctor said that since the snake only got one fang in, the "snake ring" that Rachel had given me, which blocked the other fang, probably saved my life.

My high school girlfriend was a pretty, southern belle from a solid home. I was in my senior year at Leon High School, and was "breaking in" my mother's Chevy Nova. I took Rachel fishing to wonderful St. George Island on the coast, and had one of those moments birders never forget. My spark bird was coming in from the West Indies, and I didn't even know what a spark bird was!

While standing near a small, flowering scrub oak, I noticed a small bird feeding hungrily on the tassels, obviously a warbler. I searched my mental hard drive for the species, but grinned at its colors of gold, with a garnet ear patch (the colors of my beloved FSU Seminoles). It really got next to me that I couldn't remember the species, and I could hardly wait to return home to look it up.

That night at supper, I shared with my dad about the Cape May Warbler, and had a million questions about its migration, what it was actually eating, how long it would stick around, and much more. I know now that Florida Cape Mays in late spring are quite common, but this little beauty had an uncommon effect on me. After about the fifth question, though, my father (who wanted to be listening to Walter Cronkite), told me that perhaps I should be trying to find these answers myself.

In a way, I felt that he blew me off, but soon I learned everything about bird migration I could, and I mean firsthand. I enrolled at FSU, embarking on a career which took me through about five minors, and had me cram four years of college into only six short years. The number of part-time jobs I had was only exceeded by the quantity I currently have, and the fun I was having was diametrically disproportional to my level of organization. But I had returned to birds, and in a way I never knew.

I began making trips to St. George Island that fall of 1971 with each cold front, and the number of birds these weather systems delivered was staggering. I not only loved what I was doing, this data first became Independent Research Project hours under Dr. Fran James (who took my father's position at FSU following his retirement) for undergraduate credit toward my eventual degree, and it also became the foundation for a later master's thesis.

It is hard to put a fall cold front on the Florida coast into perspective, but imagine putting up with the Florida summer sauna for several months, with the added suffering of not having any birds around to watch (to speak of). Suddenly, on one late September day, the wind begins blowing hard out of the south, the humidity becomes insufferable, and at dusk you can hardly breathe. During

the night, though, the wind shifts around to the north, the air turns crisp and cool, and at dawn there are literally birds everywhere. In the air, excitedly flying east, are Barn Swallows, Palm Warblers, flickers and kingbirds. The canopies are filled with serious warblerage, as well as their songbird counterparts from the dull vireos to some rather mysterious flycatchers. For the most part, the species flying east were headed around the gulf, and the tree feeders were trans-gulf migrants.

Each trip down I tried to break a hundred species on the island, so for the first time in my life, the number of species on a list took on some importance. My best fall day was October 10, 1976, when I recorded 128 species on the island, which is a lot for fall! My father made disparaging remarks about bird listers, and saw them as reckless, unscientific amateurs of the birding world. Needless to say, I trod lightly on this topic, and rarely mentioned the number of species I saw. But the hook had been set, and I was definitely "into" bird listing.

When I began making these trips in spring, which enabled me to structure my master's thesis around a comparison of spring and fall migration, I soon discovered that there were many more species around in spring. My father had mentioned years earlier that he once undertook a "big day" where he went out solely for the purpose of seeing how many birds he could list on a spring cold front. I'm sure this was meticulously cloaked in some scientific pursuit, but he let the cat out of the bag. He claimed 143 species that day, not too unexpected for May 5 in Florida.

My college girlfriend Bonnie and I had to try that, so following a front, we set out one April 21 and recorded 162

◄ *Eastern Kingbird*

species along the entire coastal route south of Tallahassee. Just for good measure, since we had some good birds "staked out," we tried again in two days and totaled 169 as we left for Tallahassee after dark. You cannot imagine the war hoops as a screech owl flew right in front of our windshield, narrowly missing certain death, but giving us the nice, round 170 to celebrate.

We were so excited we told Malcomb Johnson, past Editor of the Tallahassee Democrat, about it. Himself a bit of a birder, he put a small blurb in the paper, including Bonnie and me shattering my dad's record of 143. Oh, gawd; it couldn't have been worse. My purist father was plenty upset with me, like I've never seen him before or since. I didn't completely understand what was "up" with that, but I made a mental note of it, and never went there again.

THE DESERT SOUTHWEST

As much as my dad disapproved of it, the listing bug had bitten me even worse. I had now seen around 300 species

of birds, but I was growing weary of seeing only Eastern species. Spring break was coming, and I decided to go to South Texas. I studied Peterson's field guide for birds in the Rio Grande Valley, and thought of the seed that man planted in me. I also was wise enough to buy a cheap camera and lens to photograph some of the birds and other animals I was seeing.

This March spring break only afforded me nine days, so I drove all night and wound up on my brother Henry's doorstep in Houston, as usual, before they expected me there. Henry Jr. is a wonderfully kind man, deeply religious, and lives every word of it. I really regretted his moving 800 miles away before we could get to know each other, and felt guilty that I was in such a hurry. After a painfully short visit, I was blasting off for the border, in my old VW bus.

My first big life bird was majestic Whooping Cranes on the Central Texas Coast (where else?) and my spirits soared at the sight of these mammoth birds. I had always wanted to see this great survivor, and to this day believe our species deserves credit for plucking them from the brink of extinction.

Back on shore, there were Ladder-backed and Golden-fronted woodpeckers and Green Jays.

It is hard to put into words experiencing birds that you've dreamed about seeing all your life. But below Kingsville, within an hour or so, I had recorded kiskadee, Cinnamon Teal, Harris's and White-tailed hawks and the incomparable roadrunner. I was so excited I could hardly stay seated in the bus, and there were eight more days!

Late that afternoon, I drove out Boca Chica Boulevard

◀ *Whooping Cranes*

and camped in the bus out in the middle of a salt pan. I heard bird songs in the fading light that I identified as Cassin's Sparrows the next morning, when I found myself literally surrounded by Horned Larks! The odd-looking hills with handy paths yielded Curve-billed Thrashers, Cactus Wrens [no. 7] and an amazing number of Orange-crowned Warblers.

This was only a preamble to places in the valley such as Santa Anna NWR and Bentson/Rio State Park. These natural areas were loaded with new birds for me, and my life list started bulging with firsts. I worked very hard that week, sorting out a Northern Beardless-Tyrannulet, Tropical Parula, chachalaca [no.1], Botteri's Sparrow, several difficult sandpipers, and an immature Gray Hawk. I must admit, though, the young White-tailed Hawk stumped me cold, and only in recent years have I realized that bird's identity.

Driving through one small town, I was absolutely astonished to see a huge Western Diamondback Rattlesnake stretched out across the road in the early morning light. Mexican Americans were crowding around it, ready to lop its head off, and I'd never seen this species before. Trying to recall my high school Spanish, I hollered "alto" (stop) as I was scrambling out of my van. Maybe that was the wrong usage of the term, but more likely they could care less about some stupid gringo spoiling their fun in their own town. Whatever, this creature was getting a stay of execution.

Having little more than size on my side, I politely removed a long stick from one man's hands, with an apologetic "por favor," and all in one motion, I pinned down the monster snake's head, straddled it on my knees, slipped my left hand under the stick and securely behind the furious reptile's head. Barely over the deafening sound of the buzzing rattles, I remember one man's assertion of the snake's poison, by repeating "peligro" and "muy peligro" [very dangerous] over and over until I wanted to shout "silencio!" I wish I had known the Spanish words for "no kidding."

It didn't occur to me at the time that they may have wanted this creature for supper that night, but that wasn't going to happen. I carefully tossed him in a croaker sack lying on the roadside (I think this was to be his burial cloth) and deposited him in the back of my van. His destination was Boca Chica Boulevard, where I could watch him at leisure. What happened instead was what often happens when the pursuit of birds and snakes are in conflict.

I searched a town for a Tropical (Couch's) Kingbird, Inca Dove, and other South Texas specialties until noon, and then worked my way down the Military Highway for kingfishers and the like. But going back through Brownsville, being the inexperienced traveler that I was, I accidentally took the wrong road, and wound up heading to the Mexican border, and (ooops) crossed into the land of fajitas and siestas. Realizing my mistake, I immediately performed a U-turn, and was essentially reentering my country immediately.

I got out of the van to find someone to whom I could explain my error, and was gone several minutes. During my absence, apparently a female Customs Agent found my unoccupied vehicle, and decided to make an inspection.

Oh, my. She apparently slid open the side door and hopped in, this being where I walked out and felt my heart pop up to my Adam's apple. This poor woman put her hand on the burlap bag and the snake (a la any Western Diamondback) went berserk within a microsecond.

She screamed an expletive (that I dare not translate if I could) and leaped backwards and up for only about fourteen inches. At that point, the metal frame of the van took charge, and settled the age-old argument about the immovable object and the irresistible force. The thud from the back of her head was as gruesome a sound as any bug splattering on the windshield, and only slightly less fatal. She sprawled out against the back of the front passenger seat, amazingly still cognizant of the massive coils very near her.

Figuring that I would probably be executed (this is no joke in Texas these days), I tried to explain what had happened to another agent, while a third helped the woman out of my van. The look on her face bore a more-than-coincidental similarity to the one on my mother's face years ago when the cord stuck under the dishwasher turned out to be my long lost Corn Snake.

Well, as it turned out, my agent had seen me turn around, and decided there had been enough excitement for one day. I went by the female agent, as she was hovering between terror and fury, and tried to apologize. She commanded me, in the most unholy voice, to get the @#$% out of there, as well as some other choice comments, and I turned toward the van to leave. But I didn't appreciate her ugliness very much at that point, and this conflict with authority is where the wheels always fall off my wagon. However, this time I just kept my mouth shut.

The birding remained excellent for the remainder of the trip, and I will always have a fond place in my heart for the Valley. It was my first "foreign" destination, where I could hone my birding skills on the unfamiliar, and add birds to my ever-growing life list.

Car trouble, which has become routine on extended trips, first reared its ugly head on my return. As I approached Houston, my engine blew up, and had to be rebuilt in some podunk town just off HW 59. It did give me my first opportunity to commit jalapeno suicide, as well as find my first Pyrrhuloxia [no.9] and Lark Bunting. Then, with this essentially brand new motor, I was rear-ended the next day at a Pascagoula, Mississippi red light by a young woman who was – get this – breast-feeding her baby while driving! I was just thankful the infant wasn't hurt, but my equally infant motor was ruined.

With all these hardships, you'd think I'd had enough country-trotting for birds. Oh, no! It was back to work, back to school, and back to planning another excursion. My life list was nearly four hundred, and I'd even seen a few things my dad hadn't seen! However, I decided to be very low key about that with him.

Between jobs, school and playing ball, long birding trips were put on the back burner for a while. Still, the trips to the coast continued during the migration, and I felt myself getting sharper and sharper as a birder. One day, while musing through the Golden Guide with Bonnie, we began looking at all the neat new birds in Southeastern

Arizona. We decided that this would be our next big destination, the Chiricahua Mountains and vicinity.

In late spring of 1979, after the excruciatingly long wait, the drive over West Texas seemed to take half my life. As we entered Texas, the sign that said El Paso was 876 miles was deflating. And believe me, getting to San Antonio was only the beginning. Kerrville, Junction, Ozona and Fort Stockton, and we're still just half way across West Texas. Beyond Ft. Stockton there is nothing but ravens and rattlesnakes for hundreds of miles. Even entering El Paso, the beginning of the end, that sprawling city just goes on forever. I don't believe a star ship could get across West Texas in three days.

Highway 9 in New Mexico, though, was a wonderful introduction to the other side of the universe after Texas, and that road is now paved. Birds such as Curve-billed Thrasher [no.10], Blue Grosbeak and Lark Sparrow are common, with Chihuahuan Ravens nesting on many of the telephone poles. Slowing down to sub-light speed after

leaving I-10 in Texas was a refreshing experience, and the new birds began to pile up. Scott's Oriole, Black-chinned Hummingbird, and a lovely Lazuli Bunting. It was like we were suddenly in another world!

As exciting as the drive across New Mexico had been, nothing could have prepared us for the Chiricahua Mountains. We stopped early in the morning on the desert and added Lucy's Warbler, Verdin, Bushtit, Gambel's Quail and a magnificent Crissal Thrasher, to name a few. It was crisp and cool, not giving a hint of the afternoon heat to come.

Next we stopped at the famous Spofford feeder, and mopped up the lifers. Dr. Spofford was a classmate of my dad's, and even after his death, his wife continued the feeder which has blessed thousands of people with its combinations of birds. There are the two large humming-bird species, Blue-throated and Magnificent, and many Black-chinned, Anna's [no.21], Broad-billed [no.8] and Rufous [no.16]. But I also have added rare species there, including Lucifer's, Berylline and the starthroat. Still, my favorite birds were the Acorn Woodpeckers, the clown of Arizona's bird world.

It was now time for the walk up Cave Creek, the legendary haunt of trogons and many other rare Mexican stragglers and breeders. Just stepping out of the car we were mobbed by Mexican Jays, Bridled Titmice, and a whole flock of warblers and other migrants. My gosh, we added Hermit, Townsend's and Black-throated Gray warblers, Hutton's Vireo and Canyon Wren before we really got started. I was so busy scribbling life birds on my field notebook I feared missing new birds!

◀ *Acorn Woodpecker*

All these new species were great, but we both wanted to see the bird of Cave Creek: the Elegant Trogon. We walked several hundred yards, stopping for flocks, and adding life birds all the way. Then my ears picked up a call that was neither familiar to me as a species, nor even as a family. It could have been a dove, or perhaps a soft owl note; I really didn't know. Then I saw a fruiting tree in the canopy up front about where the notes came from, and I felt confident our goal was at hand. Suddenly, a bird shaped about like a cuckoo swooped through an open space and snatched a berry off a limb.

"There it is," I whispered to Bonnie. "It's the trogon!"

The bird was simply beyond reality. The metallic colors shone like a fancy car, with the red belly almost surreal. Everything about it from its eyes and bill to its long, elegant tail made it the unique bird many claim to be our country's most beautiful. I had to admit, it lived up to the hype. We sat and watched this unique creature for some time, clearly the highlight of the trip.

The climb up to the top of the mountain was both exciting and comical. We began with the air conditioner on, as it was quite warm at the bottom. As we rose in altitude, we glimpsed several neat birds in the trees. Nothing could have been more exciting, though, than the Red-faced Warbler that flew right in front of our windshield. Then, not long after that, with the air conditioner still blowing, we arrived at Rustler Park, caked with snow all over the ground. In fact, the only real warmth around was the radiator.

After camping at nearby Barfoot Park, the morning walk was nearly as amazing as Cave Creek. We added Western

Tanager, Black-headed Grosbeak [no.24], Olive and Grace's warblers, "Red-shafted" Flicker, Pigmy Nuthatch, Steller's Jay [no.11], Western Bluebird, and on and on. There were literally flocks of life birds at every corner, and abiding Yellow-eyed Juncos at our feet. Like Cave Creek, it was the place I wanted to spend the rest of my life. By the end of the day, I had also added Hooded Oriole [no.6] and Black-throated Sparrow, farther down the mountain.

From Tucson back to the New Mexico border, there are wonderful birding places dotting the map. My personal favorite, for some reason, is the rugged Guadeloupe Canyon hike. Perhaps it's the solitude it affords, or the close proximity to Mexico, but the singing Varied Buntings and squabbling Thick-billed Kingbirds don't hurt. I also found my first Violet-crowned Hummingbird (and nest) there, nearly tripping over a typically mild-mannered Black-tailed Rattlesnake. I honestly believe I could have picked that snake up without it biting, but I'm not that stupid.

This trip was also my first experience with the desert at night. During the afternoon it is so blistering hot and lifeless, I'm half expecting the Creosote to just wither and die (although I did add Western Scrub Jay and Gilded Flicker) Even around sundown it is still hot as Hades, and very little is moving. When it finally gets dark, I begin road cruising down an old road through an Indian reservation. About a hundred feet up the road is a black dot that's moving across the road. Holy cow, it's the biggest tarantula I've ever imagined!

Soon I had seen a dozen or so of the huge, hairy spiders, and other creatures were stirring. Jack rabbits hippityhopped silently over the bare ground, and the occasional kangaroo rat scurried across the road in no special hurry. This bounding species, which never drinks water, has developed the most innovative way of escaping the rattlesnake's fangs. When the snake strikes, they jump straight up and Mr. Rattler misses cleanly.

Speaking of which, by thirty minutes after dark, Western Diamondback and Mojave rattlers are crossing the road like crazy. The Westerns aren't large on the desert (like the one that introduced itself to the customs agent), but they make up for it in numbers. The very similar Mojaves are actually far more dangerous snakes, with a strong neurotoxic venom much worse than other rattlers. That is one snake I really worry about.

Soon, other species of snakes are appearing, ones I have only read about in field guides — Hook-nosed, Leaf-nosed and Long-nosed snakes, all with specialized noses adapted for burrowing in desert sand. Then, the snake that I really wanted to experience began crossing the road, absolutely unmistakable. A Sidewinder! It quite literally scooted across sideways, only contacting a small portion of its

body with the pavement at any one moment. This apparently saves them from the intense desert heat, and certainly makes them unique in the snake world.

Arizona, day or night, was a dream come true. From the low deserts to majestic Mount Lemmon, the creatures were as diverse as the habitats. Myriads of birds, interesting mammals and loads of reptiles, this extension of Mexico has vertebrates like no other place in our country. It gave me a taste of several new habitats from deserts to the high mountain, an appreciation for how animals adapt to varying conditions of temperature and aridity, and a life list of 462.

It was on my last day in Arizona, standing atop Mt. Lemmon and staring off to the North, that I knew where my next great destination had to be. I was, for all intents and purposes, at the south end of the Rockies, and I wanted more of this. Names flew through my mind like Rocky Mountain National Park, The Grand Tetons and world-famous Yellowstone. I had to go there. I had to see its birds.

THE AMERICAN WEST

During the school year of 1977-78, I took some college classes at my beloved Florida State University, worked several odd jobs, and went birding as much as possible. It certainly wasn't a career year, but I was coming close to making some progress in my future direction. I just didn't know it, because all I really cared about was a few new

◀ *Sidewinder*

birds. I saved some money and went to the coast with every cold front that spring.

Finally, though, June arrived, and I couldn't wait to load up and go. I took I-10 West to make the obligatory short visit at Henry's house, and roared out across the West Texas expanse in my new Toyota long-bed pickup. It got good mileage, could go just about anywhere, and there was plenty of room to sleep in, even though I am 6' 5". I was in heaven.

My first stop was the cavernous Grand Canyon. Golly, what a gully. The birding wasn't fantastic, although I was able to stand about six feet under a Band-tailed Pigeon, as well as seeing a lovely Yellow-bellied Sapsucker [no.18] up close. The real find of this area is a small pond several miles up the road from the north rim, which can be easily seen about a hundred yards from the road into the park on the east side.

I walked back to the pond, looking for new species of garter snakes, and settled into some low foliage on the southeast side. Never would I have guessed that I would sit there for hours, watching the thirsty birds come in to drink. Red Crossbills, Lazuli Buntings, Broad-tailed Hummingbirds [no.12], Western Tanagers, and my absolute favorite, Mountain Bluebirds. I was so close to them, and was able to squeeze off several pictures of this avian paradise.

Leaving the canyon area, I worked several parks as I picked my way north through the Rockies. My first experience with a Clark's Nutcracker was at six feet in Bryce Canyon, once called "a helluva place to lose a cow." Zion National Park had some impressive scenery, but I found it

Clark's Nutcracker ▶

somewhat lacking in birding opportunities. Beginning to
see much of the same stuff now, I accelerated to Great Salt
Lake NWR and enjoyed one of the finest birding days I
have ever known.

Entering the refuge road, I found myself gawking at
male Yellow-headed Blackbirds in the cattails not fifteen
feet away. Between their gaudy "xanthocephalus" heads
and those bizarre honking calls, they were a queer bird
indeed. With the males hovering around me at point
blank range, I think I put Kodak back into business in
about five minutes. No way I could have known that this
was only a taste of the salt lake magic that was in store!

Shorebirds, with some waders and ducks, were the order
of the day. A few sandpipers gave me some trouble, but I
was able to sort out most without too much difficulty.
What really amazed me were the numbers of phalaropes,
and I honestly had no idea how many (or maybe I was
afraid to guess). Later that day, a group of very serious
birders came by and said they estimated six hundred thousand phalaropes, and I just tried to act cool. "Yeah, that's
about what I thought." Liar liar.

Less populous but more colorful were about twenty thousand avocets and at least that number of Black-necked Stilts. They were breeding there, and put on the most amazing feign displays, contorting their bodies, wings and neck to detract attention from their eggs or young. They were also unbelievably tame, and my camera spoke early and often.

That night, camped in the hills, I discovered my life list to have exceeded 480 species, and thought about the possibility of reaching the magic number of five hundred on that trip. It would be possible, but I was beginning to realize that in order to maximize birding time (and money), I must stay on the move. Each time I repeated an area, there was little if anything new to record. Even the same habitat hundreds of miles away frequently left me looking at the same birds two or three days in a row. I pulled out my atlas and became really excited at the thought of head-

ing still farther north, to Yellowstone National Park and beyond. Why not?

I thoroughly enjoyed the drive from the Great Salt Lake to Jackson Hole. There were breeding ducks in many ponds (especially Mallards), handsome magpies seemingly everywhere, more Brewer's Blackbirds than I ever imagined, and stately Sandhill Cranes proudly marching through their pastures and fields. I felt so free, able to find new birds and indulge myself at leisure.

There's not much to Jackson Hole except the antlers surrounding the park, but I had a square meal and a badly needed shower. I still smelled like the Great Salt Lake, so a change and a good cleaning were next to godliness. The scenery along the route to the Tetons was remarkable, but the birding was only slightly above average. I did enjoy getting into a family of MacGillivray's Warblers, and couldn't believe how well they squeaked up. You gotta love the breeding season!

Despite being dead tired, I could hardly sleep that night, camping along the river. I still hadn't seen a dipper, solitaire or Golden Eagle. Something told me I was close, and that I might close the deal the next day in Yellowstone. Then I began thinking about Rosy Finches, Trumpeter Swans and Moose. Yes, a mammal. Why not? I had just that day seen a buffalo (Bison), and it was a totally grand experience. For a moment I felt depressed that my race had wiped out untold millions of these majestic creatures, and for what purpose? I tried shutting my eyes and not thinking about it, and that's the last thing I remembered.

Morning broke with a lot more than blackbirds speaking. I first tracked down a flute-like song that gave me

◀ *American Avocets*

trouble, and it turned out to be a lovely little Hermit
Thrush. It was the first time I realized how grayed out
some western birds were compared to those I was used to
in Florida. Nowhere is this more true than their close
buddy, the Veery, which I found in another location. With
robins, bluebirds and Catharus thrushes, that family was
well-represented on this day. The crown jewel came late
morning, as I walked a short trail to gaze down at the
mighty Yellowstone River. There, sitting not eight feet
from me, was a Townsend's Solitaire. Oh, my. Regrettably,
I had my camera set for scenery, with the short little lens,
and when I returned, Mr. Squeaky was nowhere to be
seen.

My biggest thrill came mid-afternoon when I spotted a
large raptor sailing off to the east, near the salt pillars. I
nearly caused a nine-hundred car pile up, but managed to
get out with the bird still visible. It clearly had dihedral
wings, but certainly wasn't a Turkey Vulture. My heart

Golden Eagle

pounded harder when I noticed the somewhat faint light
area at the base of the tail, and nearly exploded as it
wheeled, and the golden hind neck shone with the afternoon sun behind me. My knees were weak, I was sucking
air, and it was truly a deeply emotional experience, realizing I was finally gazing at a Golden Eagle. Was one life
bird better than another? You bet it was!

Yellowstone was full of surprises, too, like a Long-eared
Owl I discovered hiding in a wooded canyon. It looked
like a Great Horned Owl that got caught between two
crashing cymbals! Talk about narrow-minded. Not five
minutes later, a male Pine Grosbeak lit quite close on a
spruce, turning a simple conifer into a Christmas (comes
early) tree. Then, before it was time to find a place to bed
down, I was looking for the elusive dipper, and a splendid
pair of Common Mergansers sat like statues just across
the river from me. The fact that the late Dr. Dorothy
Dodd, Florida's retired State Librarian, had shown me one
of these on a bird count in Florida, did not in any way
detract from the pure enjoyment of seeing such a fine pair
of unfamiliar birds.

I didn't find my Trumpeter Swan until I was exiting the
area two days later, but the wait was worth it. America's
heaviest bird, its charm and grace remained with me for
several hours as I sped off to the northwest. My travel day
to Glacier National Park yielded three good looks at
Golden Eagles, but I wasn't ready to call them a trash bird
yet! Perhaps my best find was a flock of Lark Buntings,
with the males just about as handsome as black and white
can be. I have always loved the open country, and these

high plains were as gorgeous and stark as any place I've been.

Glacier National Park didn't produce many lifers, as the Rockies had already given bountifully, but a Rosy Finch later became a new bird with the splitting of the species. Still, the best bird made the drive well worth it, an adult Goshawk. I was hiking a trail, very tired, and watching out for Grizzlies. As I rounded a curve in the path, this beautiful, gray-barred missile shot across the forest opening and actually startled me a bit. My oral exuberance was a bit embarrassing, but it reminded me I was supposed to be making noise for the bears. On balance, had I been making noise, the bird may very well have never stayed for me. That thought was hard to bear..

I hated to let things like the beauty of a place get in the way of adding lifers, but I dearly loved the Road to the Sun. I would leave the entrance early morning and slowly bird my way up the road west. By midday, when it was time to make a sandwich, I would be at the top. This made it seem like I had actually taken a road to the sun, without it being there (in my face) during the climb up. That road

will always be one of my all-time favorite spots on the globe.

The third afternoon in Glacier National Park was to be my last, as I eased my way down the west side and out to civilization. From there, I took HW 2 (adding a Chukar) into Washington and across to the Seattle area. It was becoming obvious that my "Rocky Mountain trip" was augmenting. There were too many neat birds along the Pacific coast to pass up this chance, since I was "in the area."

First, I took a ferry out to Vashon Island in Puget Sound, to see old friends named the Kuperbergs. Joel was head of the Trust for Public Land, and his wonderful wife, who was working in a tofu factory, was one of the nicest people on earth. I had taught their kids a little biology in Tallahassee, and they were one of the families I most loved.

The ride over was really outstanding, as I added several alcids, such as Tufted Puffin and Pigeon Guillemot. It was great to see the Kuperbergs, too, and it gave me a chance to pal around with their youngest son, Daniel. Still, I was on a bird listing mission, and it was soon time to press on. My next destination was recommended by Daniel, for which I will always be grateful.

Taking the circuitous route, I drove out to the Olympic Peninsula and worked the national park's woodlands. This allowed me to locate some neat forest birds, perhaps my favorites being the Chestnut-backed Chickadee and the robust Olive-sided Flycatcher, both lifers. My goal was to reach this magic place Daniel described by nightfall, but between birding and the driving rain, it didn't happen.

◀ *Glacier National Park*

Nevertheless, it was a wonderful afternoon between mon-soons, as birds really come out after hard rains.

The next morning was a very special time, as I drove along the south shore of the Strait of Juan de Fuca. I did-n't think there were so many Bald Eagles in the world! There were also some neat ducks, such as Surf Scoters, but the bird of the day was a pair of Harlequin Ducks sitting right out on the rocks. I sat and looked at them for what seemed to be an eternity, and forced myself to leave. To be an effective bird lister, I decided that I needed to "get on with it" a little faster, and stop gawking at certain of the outstanding birds I was discovering for quite so long.

Adding to my sins, I couldn't resist walking out on the low tide flat, experiencing the stranded marine inverte-brates in the tidal pools. It gave me a chance to study the new Glaucous-winged Gulls, right? My favorite creatures were the sea stars, which could be garnet, red or gray. Always a solid color, they appeared to be trichromatic, a little like Eastern Screech Owls and Eastern Hog-nosed Snakes. Of course, brown screech owls are really the prod-uct of a red one and gray one crossing.

Compounding my schedule further was my desire to watch and listen to Northwestern Crows [no.19]at leisure, assessing my opinion of their relationship with American Crows. No doubt the AOU will convene a special session to listen to this youngster's observations on their taxono-my.

I arrived at my goal, Cape Flattery, late afternoon, but there was still a lot of light at this latitude in summer, so off I went. In my mind echoed those famous words, "The woods are lovely, dark and deep, but I have promises to keep. And miles to go before I reach the cape." Something like that.

The woods were lovely, dark and deep, and I now saw what was so special about temperate rain forests. There weren't many conspicuous birds to see; it was a place one had to work hard to bird. In particular, there was one rather haunting song that left me with no clue as to its identity. It was as beautiful as it was mysterious, with aberrant whistles and no special melody.

This bird had to be found! I left the trail and eased my way through the ferns and muck. Little did I know my shoes wouldn't dry until day after tomorrow, but who cared? The bird must be right up there, but where? It sang again, and by golly, it was right out in the open. Oh, man. An incomparable male Varied Thrush. How could I ever leave this rare beauty?

Back to the trail, it was now a short walk to its terminus, and all Daniel's claims were proven true. The land became nothing but a probing finger, jutting out into the strait toward Canada (easily visible on the north side). This tiny peninsula was just a few feet wide, with sheer cliffs on both sides heading straight down into the clear, blue water. And birds? Did I mention the birds?

As I walked out on the very tip, restrained by a flimsy wooden fence, a Glaucous-winged Gull sailed past me within a few feet. Almost immediately I added Western Gull, easily identified by its very dark back, almost black. Below me, alcids such as Tufted Puffins swam in the water, and I witnessed the first apparent cooperative hunt between species of my young life.

The guillemots and puffins swam underwater chasing

schools of small fish, darting this way and that. In the air, just over the water, gulls hovered to catch fish that exploded to the surface. I could be wrong, but it sure looked to me as if the alcids and gulls were working in concert, trapping their piscine meals in the water column between them. Maybe the gulls were just opportunists.

Sitting out on the very northwest tip of the United States, watching the sun set out toward the end of Canada, I felt so thankful to be alive, so in love with the outdoors, and so excited about birds. In the rapture of the moment, however, I failed to consider the walk back to the car, and found myself wandering about in this deep forest, on a very dark night, no food since a light lunch, with no light. By the time I finally emerged from the depths, those feelings of being happy to be alive were even stronger than ever.

While birding the next two days, I made an interesting discovery, at least for me. I am quite the closet salamander lover, and had looked forward to finding a few of the neat Pacific Northwest species, such as the robust Olympic Salamander. In Florida, 'manders were easily caught in their habitat by rolling logs, and grabbing them as they scamper through the leaf litter. The same is true in the Appalachians, where they actually hide under flat rocks. However, here I rolled more logs than an entire company of lumberjacks, and found no salamanders.

In reasoning this out, I decided that if they weren't under the logs, the only possibility was they were in the logs. I wasn't too confident about this hypothesis, but it was time to test it. I found a really soft, mushy log and began ripping it apart with my fingers. It couldn't have

Pacific coastline ▶

been thirty seconds before I was holding my first little squiggly amphibian, and by the time I finished that log, I found three different species and many individuals. It was literally crawling with salamanders!

It was now July, funds were running low, and it was time to begin heading in the direction of home. I drove the southern Washington and Oregon coast, just amazed at the beauty. In one place, I stopped at a convenient pull-off, and walked to the edge of the cliff. What I saw excited me more than almost any bird I had seen – it was a whale! Oh, my. I guess it was a humpback, but it was making its way down the coast, maybe two hundred yards out. I stood for several minutes watching this mighty beast surface and blow, I suppose headed for Baja California.

I was standing in a tangle of weeds in a rather unsafe place, next to a considerable drop-off. Upon looking

down, though, I was amazed to see two, no five, no at least a dozen garter snakes gathered around my position. They weren't especially afraid of me, so I snatched one up for closer examination. Naturally, the little booger latched onto my hand, and tried to get his enlarged hind teeth on my flesh. Garter snakes are bad about that. They also have a nasty saliva which can cause swelling in some humans, as a former science club president of mine named Lance found out the hard way.

Later I found that the population of garters has increased following the explosion of an introduced slug in the Northwest, and who knows what ripples in the environment that will cause. I learned later that these ubiquitous snakes also eat red land salamanders (newts to me), as well as toads. It seems they have quite a tolerance for poisonous food.

Continuing down the Pacific coastline on HW 101, the scenery remained breathtaking. I was also impressed with the Columbia River, never realizing it could be that big! It

took quite a long time to make my way down the Oregon coastline, and felt time slipping away without many new birds. Finally, I entered California, where several destinations lay before me.

After a little tourist imitation, I headed down 101 for Muir Woods and Point Reyes north of San Francisco. John Muir spent a significant amount of time in the Deep South, and I have enjoyed his writing. His woods were beautiful, and forest birding there was pleasant and rewarding. Favorite of the birds was a lovely Winter Wren feeding almost at my feet on a moist trail into the woods. There were also interesting, tiny mammals scurrying around in the debris.

The trip out to Point Reyes was incredible. I added Common Murre and Black Oystercatcher, and drove up closer to a harrier than I have ever been. Then, appearing just in front of me on a rock, was a Wandering Tattler, seemingly without a care in the world. I wound up birding this National Seashore and its nearby woodlands for two days, adding quite a good number of birds to my list.

Forcing myself to leave this exquisite area, I cut across the central valley for Yellow-billed Magpies, on my way to Sierra and Yosemite National Parks. The former will always be one of my favorite locations on earth, despite the heavy traffic that now invades the park. Wonderful rock formations simply amazed this Florida boy, where the only rocks lined railroad tracks as we took them for granite. Better than that, though, was the alpine meadow where civilization seemed to be. A walk around the entire area brought several new birds, and a definite need for oxygen.

◄ *El Capitan*

Exiting the park on the east side, I camped at Mono Lake, where thousands of phalaropes spun and dabbed all over the surface. That night I road cruised the dirt roads, and discovered no shortage of rattlesnakes strewn throughout the dry country. This was the beginning of the rain shadow, the dry area east of the Sierras, where rain clouds from the west pass over too high to drop moisture. Quite a few species of birds (anything beginning with the word "Sage") live in this arid country, but the heat of the afternoon wore on me after such a pleasant summer temperature-wise.

After feeling satisfied at my list of sage species, I returned to California by mid-July, and worked Yosemite National Park and visited the Sequoias as well. Just as I stepped out of my car at General Sherman, a White-headed Woodpecker flew up and lit right in front of me. That was an easy tick! I must say it is a staggering thought to realize that this grand old tree watched the time of Christ, and even Moses, come and go. It's amazing how easily our species can cut down an organism like that!

Leaving the parks for good, I made my way through southern California to Mt. Pinos, not too far from the asphalt monster known as Los Angeles. These were two wonderful days – the first I added some really neat birds such as Lawrence's Goldfinch and California Quail, and the second day I saw perhaps the bird of the trip. I sat for several hours atop the mountain, watching the horizon, when the huge form of my dreams floated overhead. A California Condor [no, 64]! Despite being well up in the air, it was obvious how huge this bird was, and my heart beat at least as hard as it did for the Golden Eagle. It was

THE BUDDING BIRDER : 41

not hard to believe this bird had a ten-foot wing span. This is a great mountain for birding, albeit now without condors, and I strongly recommend it for visitors to LA.

Down around the San Diego area, there were birds such as gnatcatchers that needed finding, and time was drawing dreadfully short. There were a few migrants beginning to trickle past, which led to life birds. I also took meticulous notes so that when well-differentiated subspecies such as Cassin's Vireos were elevated to species, I could add them to my life list. I spent my last night in the area with my Uncle Bill, to see how much passive cigarette smoke I could breathe in one twelve-hour period.

The next morning, it was off to La Jolla, where I had been promised Surfbirds on Black's Beach. The trip started pretty well, with good directions and fairly easy access down a dirt cliff trail. But you can imagine my surprise when, upon arriving at the bottom, I realized this was a nudist beach. Can you imagine all these folks skinny-dipping and I'm standing there fully dressed with binoculars and a camera.

Not to be defeated by my "uniqueness," I located a Surfbird (finally) and a Black Turnstone to boot. Really, I think these bathing beauties found me more odd than offensive, and come to think about it, Heaven only knows what they thought about me. It was time to leave and head for my last stop, the Salton Sea.

I splurged and overnighted in a cheap motel, just for the air conditioning. The area around the Salton Sea was really interesting, and I lucked out with two new thrashers, and great looks at roadrunners. Being more than a hundred feet below sea level was a first as well, and I knew the heat was going to be oppressive soon. Still, the refuge was productive that morning, but at noon I headed south to I-8 and east toward home. I suppose I should say I missed Tallahassee, but frankly, I was having too much fun. And my thoughts were not of home as I streaked across the desert, but rather of "where next?"

I drove like bloody heck to Arizona, where I road cruised HW 85 and 86 for much of the night. I found a Tiger Rattlesnake, Gila Monster and several Glossy Snakes, to name a few. At around midnight, I crawled in the back of my pick-up, still somewhat warm, and slept like petrified wood. Two very long days later, I rolled triumphantly back into Tallahassee, late, broke, but with 577 birds on my life list.

CHAPTER TWO

THE LAND OF THE MIDNIGHT SUN

As much as I liked my students at the Christian School, I knew there were huge philosophical differences separating me from the administration, especially the Bob Jones College product assistant principal. He could hardly live with me allowing my biology students to learn about their own bodies – like their reproductive systems – but the notion that animals have changed over millions of years was too much. You know, "evil"ution.

I have always sided with Mother Superior in The Sound of Music, when she asserted that when God closes a door, He opens a window. I left Gadsden Christian Academy in 1979, began teaching physics at Whigham High School, and more importantly, enrolled in a masters program off-campus at Georgia Southwestern College. This gave me a hunger for knowledge, the likes of which I had never known.

After a year of teaching at Whigham, home of the horrid rattlesnake round up, where they gas gopher holes to drive out rattlesnakes (and kill everything that stays in the hole), I decided to take a job beginning an alternative program in Apalachicola, Florida. I am proud that we cut the county's dropout rate in half, but reveled at the birding I was privy to. I was just across the bay from my beloved St. George Island, and I lived on Indian Pass, an outstanding location for waterbirds, with famous Cape San Blas and St. Joe State Park just around the corner. I was in Heaven!

Along the beach by my rented house, I added Mew and Lesser Black-backed gull, Pomarine and Long-tailed jaeger, Masked Booby and Curlew Sandpiper. I also fished like crazy, and had two very relaxing years. One evening, while showing my girlfriend from graduate school (who also came to Franklin County to teach) some birds in the field guide, we began looking at how incredible the birding would be in Alaska. That was when we decided to make an epic voyage that summer to the land of Eskimos and grizzlies.

My sweety's name was Cheryl Sharp, and since she sang soprano in the church choir (I was the director), her friends called her C#. She was an excellent elementary teacher, cooked Red Snapper that just melted in your mouth, and was wonderfully easy-going. That last part works well when dealing with one such as me. When summer came, my truck was about shot, and she had no money for two months. So, you can see whose car we used, and whose money.

We drove across I-10 to Texas to make the obligatory stop at my patient brother's home in Houston, and then across part of West Texas including the historic Pecos River, with its stark beauty. Cheryl was quite fond of road

Pecos River ▶

cruising, and this area near Amarillo afforded us Glossy Snakes, Long-nosed Snakes, and more rattlers than we could shake a dry mesquite branch at. We took the circuitous route, visiting the Grand Canyon, Colorado, and various parts of the Upper Rockies. We slept in the hatchback of Cheryl's Chevy, and had quite the adventure just getting to Alaska. The whole trip totaled twenty-one thousand miles, and cost me less than three thousand dollars.

This was my first real experience with longer daylight in the far North, but somehow it didn't hit me at first that this meant dawn comes earlier as well. I will never forget waking up at first light in Northern Canada and asking a passing fellow in an old pick-up what time it was, and having him say, "Quarter till three." The look on Cheryl's face was priceless.

The distance between cities in Western Canada was equally staggering. Places such as Watson Lake, Dawson Creek and Yellow Knife were hundreds of kilometers apart (and even over a thousand), with nothing in between but taiga forest. I mean, there were spruce trees as far as

the eye could see. The Al-Can Highway wasn't exactly I-10 in 1980, either, so I spent far more time dodging potholes than seeing birds. Finally, we reached the famous gold mining town of Dawson, and crossed the Yukon River to find the bonanza gold of birds.

This route took us out of the way, but I wanted to enter Alaska on the Top of the World Highway. It was really quite impressive, and had some dang fine birds, too. Sitting atop various spruces were Northern Shrike, Bohemian Waxwing and Northern Hawk Owl. What exquisite birds! That first "night" in Alaska, I did some counting, and found myself within three birds of six hundred species. I couldn't wait to see who would be the big 6 - 0 - 0.

A Willow Ptarmigan and Spruce Grouse put me one short of this temporary goal, and as the light winds and modest thermals built up, a large form rose from the trees in our path. It was a dark buteo, and I suspected a

▼ *Northern Hawk Owl*

"Harlan's" Hawk. I barreled out of the car putting my binoculars on the bird, and muttered an exuberant "yes!" It was a Rough-legged Hawk, a species I had really wanted to see.

The drive into Fairbanks was very pleasant, with creatures such as Moose and Black Bear ambling across the gravel road. There were a few new birds, but we needed a rest and a good cleaning. So did the car! We also stopped at the museum at the University of Alaska, where I met Dan Gibson. Dan is out of the old school, an ornithologist who loves finding extralimital birds and documenting them. He made (and still makes) frequent trips to Western Alaska, including islands such as Attu, and is as responsible as anyone for our understanding of rare migrants from Asia that visit our shores on occasion. Dan and I have remained friends through the years, and I have tremendous respect for his contributions to ornithology.

Feeling almost human again, Cheryl and I headed south to Denali National Park. Just walking around a little brought good luck, as my first Common Redpoll sat ten feet in front of me in the first five minutes of birding. White-winged Crossbills flew overhead, calling unceasingly, and a lovely male Pine Grosbeak lit up the spruce with his radiance. Woodland birds were abundant in Denali, and the fun was just beginning.

We decided to take the long bus ride through the park to Eichorn, seemingly at the doorstep of Mt. McKinley. At first, it was just nice scenery, with the occasional Moose to gawk at. Then, there was a small pack of wolves, which brought wonder and beauty to my day. Caribou were common, and a Red Fox ran around just outside the bus. Limiting traffic on this park road to just park-tour buses was a wise decision, and the animals are therefore tame and trusting. Near Eichorn, we actually had a Grizzly Bear walk right up to the bus door, where we sat in awe.

Birding was but a small part of the ride to Eichorn, though seeing a Gyrfalcon perched on a rock face was absolutely splendid. I like those magnificent life birds! The Dall Sheep up on the mountainside were fascinating, looking like white patches of snow. I guess that was the idea. Small ground squirrels were seemingly everywhere, but the marmots were my favorite. I thoroughly enjoyed learning about the geology of the area, as we paralleled a huge glacial moraine. I loved the distant ice fields in the mountains, lying like fluffy sheets in-between mountain peaks.

The real draw here was Mt. McKinley. From bottom to top, this is the tallest mountain in the world. It is so huge, it creates its own weather system, and many days are fairly clear, with the only clouds actually obscuring the mountain itself. On this particular day, it was fairly cloudy, and there seemed little hope of seeing the mountain. Stopping at Eichorn, I stood scanning the heavens for Golden Eagles, and happened on a huge white cloud of an odd shape, up in the air. Then it hit me, this wasn't some huge, triangular cloud at all, in was the top of Mt. McKinley! I shouted for others to look, and gasps arose in the crowd all around me. I just couldn't believe how tall the mountain was, and I will never forget those twin peaks reaching out to the heavens.

The drive down to Anchorage was rather uneventful,

but the Alpine Tundra along one stretch was especially beautiful. We were completely surrounded – 360 degrees – by the Alaskan Range, with their snowy caps forming an almost perfect circle around us. My first bird was a breeding plumage American Pipit, the first with these alternate colors I'd seen. Seeing many of Florida's winter residents in their breeding garb was one of the reasons I came to Alaska, and these buffy head-bobbers didn't disappoint me.

A careful walk through the Arctic Willows, watching and hollering for bears along the way, gave me one thrill after another. Huge, handsome Fox Sparrows sang from exposed perches, showing what beautiful birds sparrows can be. Two Golden Eagles floated effortlessly on dihedral wings over the closest summit, absolutely taking my breath away. Then, almost startling me, a male Wilson's Warbler popped up right in my face, and began his song in full voice. As I stood, completely absorbed by the birds

▾ *Mt. McKinley*

and grandeur, wind gently whistling through my hair, I knew I wanted to do this my whole life. Like so many places we visited, we had to reluctantly tear ourselves away.

Anchorage was a modern, but not unattractive city. We didn't have much to do with it, but the waterfront on the west side yielded some great shorebirds, among them being my first Hudsonian Godwits. Most shorebirds were still up on the tundra, but some were beginning to ease back to the south. There were also brant, Mew and Glaucous-winged gulls, and the bird I really wanted (OK, at that particular moment): an Arctic Tern[no.13]. It was so sleek and buoyant, with the classic dusky chest I have noticed on spring Common Terns along the gulf coast. Indeed, this bird was far more than just tick number 621.

The drive down the Kenai peninsula was as productive as it was beautiful. Just south of Anchorage, Potter Marsh is a good introduction to this great state's waterbirds. Mew Gulls busily flew this way and that, and more of those lovely Arctic Terns danced over the shallows, watching for surface-feeding minnows. But what were these swimming birds? I should have known from the cigarette butts and empty beer cans; there sat the initial Red-necked Grebe of my young life. I sat for several minutes with eyes fixed on this sharp swimmer, just thankful for being in Alaska.

Several duck species dotted the marsh as well. Very close was a pair of Lesser Scaup, notched heads and all. Finer still was a pair of Canvasback, one of the most handsome of the fowl. Quite a few Mallards attended the party, and I warily presumed them to be wild. A Short-billed

Dowitcher lit on a nearby post, looking a little out of place imitating a phoebe. In the air, Violet-green Swallows were everywhere, showing off their gaudy backs.

Potter Marsh is also a fine place to study various fish species which swim up streams to spawn, including the mighty King Salmon. The existing boardwalk not only affords additional birding opportunities, but chances to stand right above migrating fish, caught in their age-old urge to procreate their species.

Heading down the highway, the best duck appeared in an isolated pond. It was a pair of Barrow's Goldeneye. Oh, me. They mirrored each other's movements, and it seemed love was in their air. Or lust. Like so many birds in Alaska, they seemed hardly aware of us intruders, and gave me the picture that I still treasure.

Our destination that night was Seward, and we were not disappointed. It was a sleepy little town, nestled on the high bank of the Kenai fjords. Along its shore were many tourist shops, and offices for boat rides into the fjords.

This fjord was my destination, although I have always been a Chevy man. We found an out of the way driveway to nowhere, covered the car with our "darkness blanket," and fell asleep thinking of all the Kodak moments we'd seen the past few days.

The trip out onto the fjord was awe-inspiring, to say the least. Ice fields, glaciers and snowy peaks formed a backdrop of incredible beauty and majesty. Bald Eagles sailed over like so many Fed Ex commercials, often drawing the ire of Northwestern Crows. It was a little rough on the water, but few noticed with all there was to take away our attention.

My favorite part of the trip bird-wise was the colony of Black-legged kittiwakes. One of several life birds at this rocky cliff, these noisy chaps constantly flew by with their unmistakable "dipped in ink" wings. There were also alcids, a family I'd had only fleeting experience with, coming from Florida. Common Murres were indeed abundant, making the best penguin imitation of any alcid. Joining them were Rhinoceros Auklets, a sporty little fellow near the boat, and Pigeon Guillemots. One Horned Puffin joined the Tufteds, apparently being somewhat out of place. Pelagic Cormorants were everywhere, but the unearthing of a Red-faced became the talk among another bird-watching couple. There were other birds too, but the mammals seemed to take the spotlight at this point.

The first of the trifecta were several Sea Otters floating on their backs, with pups in tow. The "what, me worry?" look was absolutely darling to Cheryl, and I must admit a fondness for them. Farther out into the mouth, it got rough, but just as we contemplated turning around, the cry of "Orcas" rung from the captain's loud speaker. Sure enough, two modest fins and the obvious tall fin of the

◄ *Colony of murres and Kittiwakes*

male protruded from the water's surface like stakes in a field. I couldn't believe I was standing there looking at Killer Whales!

We putted out into the open Gulf of Alaska, and turned around to head for home. At about this time, the captain announced that a humpback had been spotted at some location north of us, toward the dock, and we went searching. Cheryl and I stood wide-eyed on whale watch, clearly captivated by the avian and mammalian miracles of the day. Just as she was saying how perfectly satisfied she was with the day, the huge form of a humpback shot out of the water like an Apollo rocket, breeching clean out of its briny home, and crashing down sideways with a force that sent water spewing in all directions. Welcome to Alaska.

The Sitka Spruce forests in this area were deep, cool places for northern songbirds. Everywhere I looked there were neat birds, such as Gray and Steller's jays, Hammond's Flycatchers, Orange-crowned, beautiful Yellow-rumped and Townsend's warblers, peerless Golden-crowned Sparrows, flutist Hermit Thrushes, Pine

Sea Otters ▼

Siskin and the indescribably magnificent Varied Thrush. Many were new birds for me, but most were as delicious as they were unfamiliar. It sure beat summer in North Florida.

The drive down to the southern tip of the Kenai peninsula was scenic and pleasant. My favorite part was the last few miles, with huge, snowy mountain peaks off the west edge, with this area being quite the cliff. We camped overlooking this breathtaking view, and awoke to the subtle songs of Orange-crowned Warblers, Northwestern Crows croaking and various chickadees chattering. Famous Homer Spit awaited us, but nothing could have prepared me for this awesome area.

From the city of Homer, a long, artificial peninsula creeps out into the gulf like a probing finger. It is largely rocky on the west side, but has a nice mud flat on the eastern cove. One of my first birds was a Yellow-billed Loon about sixty yards out to the west, a bird that I have seen there on subsequent trips. In 1995, I found a Black-tailed Gull right there on shore, so I have learned that the base of the peninsula is quite good for birds on both sides.

Bald Eagles are all over the spit, and unbelievably tame. There are also lots of gull, sea otters, and many surprises such as Bar-tailed Godwit, eiders and other sea ducks. The very end of the spit finds a parking lot on the left side, where birders can actually sit in their car (on cold days) and watch the parade of sea birds fly by. Guillemots, puffins, auklets, gulls, ducks and cormorants lead the pack, and one can compose quite a list with little effort. Birds were also quite tame, and one Tufted Puffin fed below us with total lack of concern.

Tufted Puffin ▶

The rocks on the west side of the base are covered with barnacles, and attract Surfbirds, tattlers, and Black Turnstones, to name a few. June is not as good as May or July and August, but there is no perfect window in Alaska for all birds. June is the best month on the tundra, but the slowest for shorebirds on the south coast. That gives us a good excuse to spend the whole summer there, or to go back to Alaska over and over. Indeed, I seem to have done the latter.

Evidence of the 1964 earthquake may be easily seen in this area. Some destruction remains, but odd images like sewer pipes sticking out of sheer cliffs with no place to go, assure the observer that something really big happened years ago. Low areas of spruce were flooded with salt water, virtually preserving the trees like petrified wood. Other stands of dead spruce are the result of cold winters, when porcupines had little else to eat but tree bark.

Regrettably, cold winters are more a thing of the past in this area, and the forest is paying for it. A species of beetle is controlled by typical cold winters, but global warm-

ing has been a boon for this insect. It is sad that the beetle's good fortune has raised their population exponentially, and the spruce forest is suffering dearly. I am constrained to say that when our species begins altering global weather patterns, it is time to take a long look at our activities.

With some hesitation, Cheryl and I left the Kenai peninsula having seen a great section of Alaska, and wishing only to see more. The highway running east from Anchorage passes parallel to more of the Alaskan Range, and affords stupendous views of one of the world's truly great chains. Taking the road south on Highway 4, we made good time for Valdez, and its lovely birding areas.

Our first stop was Thompson's Glacier, where we heard Golden-crowned Sparrows almost before climbing out of the car. It was a very birdy area, as well as a nice stop for tourists. My best find here was a White-tailed Ptarmigan, well outnumbered in this state by the Willows (Alaska's State Bird), as well as Rocks, which are plentiful in their outcrop habitat.

Valdez, the "Little Switzerland," is a remarkably beautiful town, with great birding opportunities. The marsh approaching from the north is full of birds and fish, with scattered Moose. A drive west from town, now being somewhat developed, yielded a pair of tame Harlequin Ducks, one of my most coveted birds.

Last, the road around the east side of the bay was exquisite, with many neat waterbirds and a fairly close nest of Bald Eagles. I must say, my first experience with young Bald Eagles, so light underneath, sent me pouring over my field guide! Valdez is somewhat out of the way, but those with time will find it rewarding for birds and scenery.

The highway along the Copper River was a typical "Alaska scene" with high mountains and grand views. There are many small roads leading away from the main highway, and these were quite productive on my first trip, and subsequent ones. One of the birds I most wanted to see in Alaska, because of its taxonomic uniqueness in America, was the Arctic Warbler. After several hours of looking through neat sparrows and other songbirds, this Old World species began singing in a willow about thirty feet away. I suspected it might be this species, almost by elimination, but I was really excited to finally land this "big one."

We also worked Highway 8, which was better for birds than tires. Acting on some advice, I located a Smith's Longspur after about an hour of searching. I've always loved longspurs, but this rarity had to that point escaped my binocs. Soon, I had a singing male within ten feet, and found myself staring obliquely, ignoring the horde of mosquitoes around my head. In every way, I guess I had been

◄ *Nest of Bald Eagles*

itching to find this bird, and it was not in vain. Returning to the car, we found very tame Pine Grosbeaks [no.22].

At this point, we had driven just about every mile of road in Southern Alaska, below Fairbanks, and we both knew what lay before us. We had talked about the North Slope Haul Road, or its new name, the Dalton Highway. It was a bad road, getting worse each mile one foolishly travels north of Fairbanks. Cheryl and I had the same conversation we had months ago, where we discussed what havoc this leg of the journey could have on her new car. The result was the same.

We bought food — a lot of food — in Fairbanks, took about three showers, and headed north. At first, it wasn't so bad, so we hoped against hope that it had somehow improved. Fat chance. In the beginning, there were some potholes in the pavement. Then, there was some pavement framing the potholes. By the third hour, we had long since forgotten what pavement looked like, and found the gravel road not that bad. It was like the Al Can.

We stopped for gas at the Yukon River, and had to play "North to Alaska" one more time. I swear, if I heard "we crossed the Yukon River, and found the Bonanza gold" for another reprise, I was going to drive off into the spruce forest. I must say, the initial view of this huge, glassy river is an unbelievably beautiful scene, cutting through the taiga forest with gentle strength. This was only exceeded by the Star of Bethlehem that sat upon a huge spruce tree when the light got low. This star has a huge, brown body, a big round head, and monster eyes. It was nothing at all but a Great Gray Owl. I was so excited to get that big fella's picture, albeit in low light.

Yukon River ▶

The next day, we reached the tiny village of Coldfoot. There, we gassed up, took a shower, and had the pivotal experience of the entire trip. Several Alaskans approached us in front of the café, asking us what our plans were. When we told them, they issued the longest streak of pessimism I have ever heard, ending with the promise that "we'd never make it." Then, one chimed in, "alive."

The biggest problem was the cut shale used to line the roads, and how it loves to cut tires like a hot knife through butter. But they also reiterated several times that our little car could never make it up Attigan Pass, because of the deep mud and steep angle. It was impossible. Plain and simple. Open and shut. Forget it. No way. End of chat.

Respecting Cheryl and her car, I turned south upon exiting Coldfoot, and headed toward Fairbanks. I wanted Cheryl's honest reaction — and I got it! "Gee - um" (that was South Georgia for "Jim"), "what are you doing?" I looked at Cheryl with a dead straight face and said the men convinced me it was too difficult and dangerous to

attempt the second half of the haul road. What followed spoke volumes about what lay inside my special friend:

"We've driven thousands of miles . . . for what? You're turning around because four fat old bearded men are jealous that we have the courage to face those obstacles? You turn my car around and put the pedal to the metal!"

Obviously, trucker's lingo was the rage at that time. But what a woman!

I wish Attigan Pass had been closer, because I was sweating the encounter. Still, we passed through many miles of beautiful taiga forest, with occasional lovelies such as Northern Shrike atop the spruces. We also had an incident that irks me to no end every time I think about it. I was driving along about 40 mph, and looked up out my side window to check out a bird I passed. I watched it for several seconds, and determined that it was one of forty million stupid robins we'd seen that day. It was at this time that Cheryl interrupted the silence and said, "Gee-um, I just saw a great big black dog run across the road right in front of us. Now whatcha 'spose he's doin' out here?"

I can't believe I missed a melanistic Gray Wolf for a robin.

Soon after that lovely incident, we arrived at one of the beautiful places in Alaska, and one that has magic all its own. It's up on a rise of elevation, with a rocky outcrop on the right side of the road. Nearest the road are four extensions of granite curving out together from the ground, about eight feet tall. This gives the location its name, Finger Mountain. There's a nice parking area, and several very interesting birds. Here, I found some Rock

Ptarmigan, waddling off like ducks to water. Finger Mountain also overlooked a huge glacial valley known as Old Man Camp, with an abandoned airstrip and ditches created by borrowing soil to raise the air strip.

We drove down to the valley and off the road onto the airstrip. Standing to my left was a shorebird, and almost immediately I realized I was looking at a whole family of Bar-tailed Godwits. Those chicks were so cute, and the parents were quite agitated. My camera flashed like lightning, and the birds were immortalized. I don't believe I will ever tire of taking pictures of great birds.

While I was staring at the godwits, a small bird appeared in an Arctic Willow in front of me. After careful observation and use of the field guide, I concluded it was a Hoary Redpoll. Suddenly, the ditch produced a Green-winged Teal with chicks, and watching them led me to another life bird: an American Tree Sparrow. Cheryl and I drove slowly around the airstrip and found quite a few neat northern birds, as well as mosquitoes so large, they had to file flight plans just to take off.

Back on the road, that sinking feeling began to well up inside of me again. It was like impending doom. I knew we were in for a battle at Attigan Pass, and I was not at all convinced we were going to conquer its heights. It wasn't about self-doubt, it was about the very laws of physics I taught at Whigham High. Some things are just impossible, and that's all there is to it. But in case you're wondering, if I were by myself, you can bet I would have headed straight for the pass. Those old boys meant well, but many people are just melodramatic and sensational, often not taking into account the desire and persistence of others. Or their arrogant stupidity.

We arrived at the Brooks Range early afternoon. Before us, it loomed like a huge barrier to where we wanted most to be, somehow keeping us from what we wanted to become. There were no windows, so if God closed this door, that was it. All or nothing. And maybe, now or never.

The road was its usual decent self right up to the beginning of the incline. Unfortunately, the weather was not our friend. A low pressure cell had been sitting over central Alaska for a week, and we hadn't seen the sun in days. As this moisture, presumably off the Gulf of Alaska, met the Brooks Range, it rained profusely. So needless to say, the road up was a mess. Deep mud and unearthed, cut shale. We weren't going to make it.

I dropped the car into first gear, let out the clutch, and drove into the crud at about fifteen miles per hour. The pretty little red car made it about fifty feet and no more. It bogged down, wheels spinning on flat shale caught in the ooze. With Cheryl driving and me pushing from the front, we managed to back it down to the flat bottom and I nearly died from exhaustion. I lay there on the wet dirt, mosquitoes buzzing me, and Cheryl standing over me saying, "Let's try it again."

OK. I backed up about one hundred feet and gunned it up pretty good. We hit the swamp in second gear, at maybe thirty-five mph. Mud flew everywhere, rocks crashed underneath, and the tires squalled on hunks of rock. At the fair, we pay good money for rides like that. But, in the end, the result was the same. This time, we got about two hundred feet, and slowly gave in to gravity and little friction. I must tell you, I was gaining some ambivalence about eiders and phalaropes.

Pushing the car back down on my hands and knees, I was caked with wet mud from head to toe. My shoulders ached from pushing with all my might, my knees were torn up from the shale, and I was acutely aware that we had skipped lunch. I have to tell you, I felt sorry for myself. But looking up, there was Cheryl again. I guess I don't have to tell you what she said.

We agreed, this third try was "it." The seventh game of the series. Win or lose, we go on or go back. No more speeches from the brave girl. No more foolish stunts from the guy. We were prepared to give it our best shot and let the shale chips fall where they may. And oh, did they!

Needless to say, we got quite a running start, hitting the Mutarin Nebula between fifty and sixty mph in fourth gear. It was like a passing bomb hitting, with a rock explosion only matched by the array of airborne mud from Canada to Russia. The windshield was brown, the engine racing, and there was hope.

I downshifted to third about where we first got stuck, and similarly dropped into second even with where we dug out of the second car-swallowing bog. We were losing our rev, though, and finally I hit first gear several hundred yards up the mountain road. It was still soft and gooey, though, and I feared the end was near.

It was. I was truly crushed when our progress was halted. Cheryl kept quiet, as she had good instincts about men. I pulled my muddy boots off the pedals and plopped them down in the mud. I couldn't believe I was going to have to push this car all the way down to the bottom. And if I was to clean up at Coldfoot, you know who'd be the first people we'd see. Oh, man, this wasn't a vacation, it was an ordeal.

As I stood there, maybe expecting a star ship to come along to help us (there sure wasn't anyone else), it occurred to me that the water in the soil must be pulled by gravity like everything else. So, I walked up the mushy road a little way and felt it more solidly under my feet. I saw out of the corner of my eyes Cheryl watching me, so I walked down to include her. I gathered myself, and shared my thoughts, "We won't go down and try again, but . . ."

"I'll drive; you push," she said confidently, and pointed up the road. Truly, a superior woman.

I knocked off a few large pieces of shale, played squeegee with my boots between the ruts and in general, made the road slightly more passable. Then, we eased the car down a tad, and put the biggest piece of flat shale we could find under the tires. I gave a few last minute instructions to Cheryl, and counted, "one, two, THREE!"

The car began moving slowly uphill, tires screaming their grooves off. The "opposite and equal reaction" Newton promised was a steady stream of mud all over me, especially when I got down on my hands and knees. I could tell I was making a difference, because every time the car got out of reach when I was on all fours, it virtually stopped. And then, imperceptibly at first, it moved under its own power. It kept moving — it was almost beyond belief, but we made it!

Cheryl stopped two hundred yards uphill, as I instructed her, and that was the longest two football fields this former wide receiver ever trudged. Looking down at the quagmire that let us out of its grasp, I honestly was in disbelief that we weren't still there, starving to death. In what seemed funny at the time, I looked at Cheryl and said, "See, it's like what the Mother Superior said on The Sound of Music, when nature closes a door, kick it open."

If the feeling we had at that moment was triumph, it would be hard to describe the words for the final ascent to the top of the Brooks Range at Attigan Pass. We reached an altitude where the clouds and rain were behind us, and broke over the top, where it was sunny and completely clear to the north as far as we could see. That includes seeing the Arctic Sea well off in the distance. We were ready for Heaven, because we'd had enough of the other place.

Attigan Pass was a truly mountaintop experience. The first bird we saw was a beautiful male Snow Bunting, looking like something from Alaska's Arctic. Common Ravens were croaking in the distance, and then a boldly-patterned bird lit lightly upon a rock. It was a wheatear. Oh, that was so rich. Then, one of my most favorite birds came hopping along the montane tundra, a Gray-crowned Rosy-Finch. He was so tame and abiding, but caused me to gush excitement and emotion.

Attigan Pass has a stark beauty all its own. Peaks modestly covered with snow drifts outline the sky, while barren mountainsides lay strewn with rocks. Every winter the deep freeze busts more and more of the mountains to till, with ice its major force of erosion. Below us to the north, the road wound slowly out the canyon, downslope to the coastal tundra. The promised land.

For the remainder of our time north of the Brooks Range, we never saw a cloud. I believe the mountains inhibited the weather over central Alaska from moving north, allowing us to have both sunny days and sunny nights. I did have fun with Cheryl, when we bedded down and I started out for a short walk. She asked me when I was coming back, and I said "before dark."

The next morning we eased along the haul road, within easy distance of the pipeline itself. In one of the high points of the trip, I photographed a Gyrfalcon sitting on the pipeline, as well as a jaeger, Golden Eagle and Glaucous Gull. I also took shots of an Arctic Fox and Caribou underneath the pipeline, with Cheryl leaning against it. The scenery, including the bizarre Franklin Bluffs, was simply extraordinary.

We slowly worked down to the pump station which was our destination for the day. We had to be careful, as a grizzly was out roaming the tundra. An attack was very unlikely, but erring on the side of caution is something I do

▼ *Snow Bunting*

(about once a year). This area toward the end of the river valley was to become my favorite place on earth, beginning with the events of the next two hours.

The row of Arctic Willows alongside the road was full of birds, though only a few species. Both Hoary and Common redpolls were abundant, and the double note of the commons easily came back to me from a few days prior. Joining the redpolls were White-winged Crossbills, giving me great looks at a bird I'd always wanted to see. Adding to the excitement and high-pitched vocalizations were several Yellow Wagtails, a brand-new group to this still-young birder. It was after a good look at a wagtail that I realized what an incredibly memorable moment this was.

As we moved out from the last of the canyon, there were fewer land birds and more water birds on the flat, coastal tundra. Many birds simply made my heart race: an incubating American Golden Plover, a pair of Surf Scoters, Arctic Terns [no.13], Red-throated Loon, Red [no. 20] and Red-necked phalaropes, Long-tailed Jaeger [no.23],

 Gyrfalcon

Greater White-fronted Geese, Short-eared Owl and several sandpipers. The list just went on and on.

I could have driven that road to Prudhoe Bay umptidump dozen times, and still seen new birds. Wow, there's a Snowy Owl! Oh, man, a Pomarine Jaeger. Look, a Red Phalarope! Had I to do it over, we would have spent an extra day there, but I have this habit of moving on too fast, I think.

Upon arriving at Deadhorse, close to the Arctic Sea, we drove around looking in kettle ponds, and found some wonderful birds like male King Eider, a family of Spectacled Eiders, loads of Long-tailed Duck, exquisite Pacific Loons, scoters, Sabine's Gull and many sandpipers. My favorite bird, in a way, was the displaying Pectoral Sandpipers, letting their shaggy chest feathers bizarrely puff out. To this day, I will never look at a Pectoral Sandpiper in the same way.

We drove up to the gate at Prudhoe Bay, and the guards

could hardly believe their eyes. They could not believe we'd made the trip up from Fairbanks. They all agreed that to the best of their knowledge, we were the first two-wheel drive car to ever make the trip! We were really a bit of a novelty, but I guess they don't get that much excitement up there at the end of the universe.

They didn't know exactly what to do with us, since we just kind of drove up like we had some kind of appointment into this restricted area. But I just acted like I belonged there, so they called their naturalist, a wonderful older man named Angus Gavin, and we hit it off really well. He was quite knowledgeable, and seemed attracted to the adventure in our eyes.

Angus not only gave us free reins around Prudhoe Bay (something you'd never get today), he also invited us to ARCO's dinner that night. Honestly, I have never seen so much food, before or since. Steaks, seafood, fruit, veggies, everything fresh and delicious. We ate like hogs, and had to put air in the tires just to drive to camp. Between visions of Arctic birds, the car being bright as noon day, and feeling like I had the last six Thanksgivings inside me, sleep was not an option.

Cheryl and I covered the entire Prudhoe area the next couple of days, and saw the magic of Alaska. I honestly don't know how many thousand Long-tailed Ducks there were on the Arctic Sea, but it was a staggering sight. We saw a Polar Bear out on the ice floes, a mother Grizzly with three cubs, Arctic Caribou [no.68]wandering all over the oil fields, and the State Bird (Willow Ptarmigan) seemingly escorting us through the property. Truly, these sights were the stuff of dreams.

◀ *Long-tailed Jaeger*

Since that time, Angus has gone on to the Great
Refinery in the Sky, and the oil companies have virtually
closed their land to the public. Indeed, much has changed
in the last quarter-century. The haul road has been
improved, though parts are still pretty bad, a few more gas
stations have been added, and truckers are decent folks
who frequently stop and help the few loco tourists who
brave the Dalton. Still, there will always be something
very special about this land "way up north" and it is the
only place on Earth I absolutely cannot stay away from.
There are a million sane reasons for going anywhere but
the Dalton, but the inescapable pull of Arctic birds in
their element has now brought me back five summers, and
I wouldn't bet against many more.

As it was, I didn't return to Alaska for nearly ten years,

◄ *Willow Ptarmigan*

finally with the woman I eventually married. We repeated many of the same destinations, but included Western Alaska, around Nome. By this time, my life list was considerably higher, since I had been to many other countries. But I wanted to reach the magic plateau of seven hundred species for North America, as defined by the ABA (not geographers), and I was close.

Having just rented a wreck, one of the first birds we found was a White Wagtail, life bird number 698 for North America. It was a lovely little bird, with the telltale bobbing head and high-pitched calls. With some searching, we found a Bristle-thighed Curlew, which brought me to the verge of my goal. Then, working along the shoreline, stood a Rock Sandpiper, number seven hundred. I

◀ *Rosabelle Stevenson in front of Mt. McKinley*

felt pretty satisfied, but in all honesty, I enjoyed the curlew a lot more. What was wrong with me?

Years passed again before I returned to Alaska, but did so in 1995, with thirteen wonderful students of mine. Then, in 2001, I took my 83-year-old mother, who'd hardly ever been on a vacation. This was a great trip, as we saw bears, whales, "the" mountain on clear days, and I took my first trip up to Barrow. I actually saw a life bird, a Steller's Eider. Finally, in 2002, I led my first professional trip to Alaska, with nine clients, several of them close friends.

Alaska is different from every other place on earth. Its size, grandeur and rugged nature make it special in so many ways. There are some of the neatest, most unique birds in all the world, and fantastic mammals as well. Then, there's the twenty-four-hour daylight, which must be experienced to be understood. Despite what Dorothy said about "home;" in my opinion, there's no place like Alaska.

CHAPTER THREE

TRIALS IN THE TROPICS

Believe me, traveling to other states is nothing like operating in different countries. Listening to the way New Englanders talk cannot compare to trying to understand Spanish, especially when your Spanish teacher in college spoke Castillian. Riding over some rough Alaskan roads hardly prepares you for the path through the forest called the Pan Am Highway. Having to keep an eye on your valuables at Walmart pales in comparison to a country where stealing is just a way of life. Putting up with a few selfish drivers in East Texas who don't know or care that the left lane is for passing, cannot hold a candle to the lead-footed, suicidal maniacs that race along Mexican highways like there is no tomorrow. Regrettably, all too often, there isn't.

My least favorite thing about the tropics is the noise levels. Many automobiles compete with Apollo Rockets for decibels (not to mention the fumes), dogs bark all hours of the night (drowned out by roosters pre-dawn), children running the streets until midnight scream constantly, music blares from stereos in many directions, and the constant chorus of car horns is enough to unnerve even the most seasoned driver.

Unfortunately, there is also nothing like Mexican birds, and the farther south one goes, the better the birding gets. This is what I realized while thumbing through my Uncle Buck's (Ernest P. Edwards) books on Mexican birds. Feeling like I had pretty well conquered all lands north of the Rio Grand, I began looking for my next excursion, and Mexico was readily accessible with my brand new Toyota diesel pickup.

Uncle Buck's books really fired me up. First, I glanced through the color plates, and my bird brain started salivating at the thought of seeing motmots, more trogons, parrots, oodles of tanagers, all the orioles, honeycreepers, manakins and possibly a Lovely Cotinga or even a quetzal! I also wanted the challenge of sorting out antbirds, woodcreepers and little green flycatchers. Truthfully, I think I was a little bored with United States birds, and they were becoming awfully easy to identify. More than that, I was fast approaching thirty, and my life list wasn't going anywhere.

These sorts of trips also get expensive, so I organized an expedition with seven boys I had known in the camps I ran most summers. The snakes of Mexico were as attractive as the birds, and these kids were snake hunters through and through. I would wear my binoculars and check off new birds as I saw them. We put my truck on a tow bar behind my first school bus (named Martha), and steamed away one hot August morning in 1978 for points south of the border.

After turning my brother's back yard into a pin cushion with tent stakes, we drove through blistering South Texas and crossed into Mexico as carefree and excited as we could be. Much of northern Mexico is dry wasteland, so we headed down the gulf slope toward Tampico. The habitat changed and we began our field work. The boys combed the grasslands and woods for snakes, and we soon discovered that Mexico had a lot of really fast serpents. These relatives of our racers, coachwhips and whipsnakes were diurnal, very alert, and fast as greased lightning. It was quite amusing to watch my little band of "we never miss" egos get whipped so frequently by dumb reptiles.

My luck was better with birds. We worked some natural areas around El Naranjo, and I soon added a Thicket Tinamou walking right in front of me as we combed the bushes for snakes. One of the kids spotted a Tamaulipas Pygmy-Owl almost hidden in a tree, and we all got a kick out of seeing some Military Macaws. One quite tame Gray Hawk perched very close on a nearby tree. The truth is, I was adding birds to my life list so fast I couldn't keep track. In the three days we worked this area, I checked off fifty-seven new birds.

The fourth day we backtracked to Gomez Farias, at an earlier suggestion by my dad. We saw lots of birds, and quite a few neat snakes, including varieties of coral snakes. Some of my more memorable birds from this day included Blue Mockingbird, Crimson-collared and Hooded grosbeaks, Singing Quail and Gray-collared Becard. I couldn't believe I'd already seen over seventy life birds!

We moved south toward Yucatan, but opted to spend some time in the Veracruz area at Uncle Buck's suggestion. On the way, we found some freshwater marshes on a side highway to Tecolutla, and they were full of birds and snakes. The boys really enjoyed such conspicuous birds as tiger-herons, wild Muscovies, crakes, Lesser Yellow-headed Vulture, and a marvelous Boat-billed Heron. That was nothing compared to their excitement over road cruising for snakes along the road into town that night.

Even before the sun set, snakes were out on the road. Warning flags went up when a cantil, a Mexican "moccasin," lay out on the shoulder, just looking for someone to bite. By the time the sun had set, we had already seen four species of snakes, with the best clearly yet to come. With our huge Q-beam spotlight, we were able to look into the ditch as well, having the snakes at a clear disadvantage. We also got a great look at a Yellow-breasted Crake, as well as a King Rail. During our cruising, we saw two boa constrictors, various assorted rattlesnakes, a beautiful

▼ Gray Hawk

kingsnake that mimicked coral snakes, and a bunch of smaller varieties. Needless to say, the spirits of the boys were sky high. That was a hard spot to leave.

We had some good birding around Cordoba, and enjoyed getting out of the heat for two days. There aren't as many snakes in the mountains, but the kids were happy with anything. Then, we returned to the lowlands and began working our way southeast again. We would do a lot of walking in the morning, eat lunch and drive most of the afternoon, and road cruise for snakes after supper. It got to be a routine, and everyone was having a great time.

The second morning down in the lowlands, though, we had an experience that frankly, none of us believe. We were walking eight abreast across an open grassy woodland, rolling old logs for critters and seeing some neat new birds. I had just added Masked Tityra and Fork-tailed Flycatcher [no.32] when one of the boys hollered "snake"

Boat-billed Heron ▼

in a tone that made me know he had a good one. Running was not allowed, but we soon gathered and formed a circle around the spot the young man claimed the snake stopped.

Everyone was instructed to watch the area in front of them, and to be ready for anything. Several minutes passed, and to my shock, the head of an absolutely monstrous caribo raised up from the tall grass. There was no mistaking this "indigo snake" – a harmless species with an affinity for chewing the head off poisonous varieties. Catching this fellow would be the quetzal of snakes, and this one was in the bag. I mean, I had seven terrific little snake hunters surrounding the huge serpent, so what could go wrong?

We eased closer until just about every kid could fall on the snake. I reminded them that this was an extremely fast snake, and this big fella didn't get so large by being stupid. There was about eight feet of snake, and all anyone had to do was grab any part of it, and this terrestrial leviathan was ours. So, on the count of three: One, two, THREE!

Folks, to say we didn't catch the snake would be an understatement. We don't even know which way it went. As we dove, there was a whirring in the middle of the circle, and this huge blackish reptile vanished before seventy fingers hit the ground. The kids all lay there looking at each other. "Have you got it?" "No, I thought you did." "Naw, I never saw it." It was all too funny.

My little band of terrors got up sheepishly and quietly dusted themselves off, pulling grass and other vegetation out of their hair. We went about our snake hunting a bit more humble, and never forgot the lesson that creature laid on us in the sweltering humidity.

We spent two more days in these Mexican gulf lowlands, birding and snaking in the morning, moving south by afternoon, and cruising the night's first two hours. Although the trip had gone well so far, trouble struck on the highway from Coatzacoalcos to Cardenas. Zipping along the main road, the engine of the bus suddenly went klunk. I knew before any cursory inspection that we just broke down big-time, and we were a long way from home.

I found a cheap hotel nearby, and got the kids situated in several rooms. Then, a mechanic towed the bus to his shop, and said it would be ready in two days. In the meantime we worked these lush lowlands using my truck, such as around Las Choapas, and saw an impressive collection of birds. Added to my list were such lovelies as Rufous-capped Warbler, Red-throated Ant-Tanager, Red-capped Manakin [no.54], Little Hermit and the incomparable Montezuma Oropendola. Road cruising for snakes, we also saw Mottled Owl and Spot-tailed Nightjar.

The news got much worse when I returned to claim the bus and everyone acted like they had no idea what I was talking about. They stole it. It was absolutely gone, and we weren't seeing it again. We all just stood there, jaws dropped in disbelief that an entire place of business could so brazenly steal our vehicle. Man, where was the Florida Highway Patrol when you needed them!

At least I had the wisdom to have removed our belongings before leaving the bus with those guys. We had tents, sleeping bags, and my truck. We piled our stuff in the back, and the kids sat on them. It was quite comfortable, and the weather was remarkably dry for August in the tropics. There was a reason for that, which Mr. Meteorology here was going to be slow to grasp.

My inclination was to head back, but that was met with unanimous, serious opposition. So, we eased our way into the state of Tabasco, and onto the Yucatan peninsula. Gone were the lush rain forests, but there were many new birds and the snake hunting was incredible. Our first night, we road cruised until well after midnight on an old road through the forest, seldom going a mile before the next snake. There were big boas, Cat-eyed Snakes, Lyre Snakes, Night Snakes, and some rat snakes I couldn't identify. On the hot side, there were four species of coral snakes, several rattlesnakes and a whopping Fer-de-lance. In all my years of snake hunting around the world, this monster ranks as the meanest looking creature I have ever encountered. He was hideous.

There was a lot of endemic birds I tried to find in the Yucatan, and most are relatively common and easily seen. They're easy to find in field guides, too, as their names all seem to start with "Yucatan." My favorite had to be the beautiful Yucatan Jay!

The kids were pretty ambivalent about the ruins, although it's hard not to be impressed with some of the structures. Overall, we enjoyed Yucatan a lot, but had to depart before we intended.

It seemed there was trouble brewing in the tropics. I had noticed an awful lot of snakes moving, even in broad daylight. Added to that, I couldn't help seeing quite a few flocks of birds heading west, off the Yucatan. It also got very overcast and windy, which was beginning to bother me. At that point, I found a radio station and walked in to get a weather report. I will never forget this cordial but very professional gentleman looking at me and saying, "The largest hurricane out of the Atlantic this century is bearing down on us."

Gulp. Here I am with seven kids and a small pick-up, and a monster storm headed our way. In my own carefree way, I walked out to the truck and asked the troops if they would like to head for the high country, and leave the heat of Yucatan. There was no argument.

We loaded up and drove west, off the Yucatan, and into the mountains of southern Mexico. Birding was excellent, and the hurricane demolished parts of Yucatan. I called the phone committee to let them know we were fine, and they seemed relieved. Forgot to mention about the bus. Now, twenty years later, I might have handled that situation a little bit differently.

With a few days of driving, we reached the United States border, where we mobbed the first McDonald's we could find. The hurricane had struck there as well, and most of South Texas was underwater. I will never forget driving up the desert highway toward Kingsville, and having a Sooty Tern fly across the road in front of us. We returned to Tallahassee two days later, never having had the first drop of rain fall on us. But yes, I know how lucky we were.

In 1979, I visited a small, private school named Gadsden Christian Academy, to set up a summer camp for kids interested in snakes, birds and other goodies. The principal was a kind man named Larry Dubose, who quickly agreed to the plan. Then, my whole life took a major turn when he added that they were also looking for a "good science teacher." I distinctly remember opening my mouth to say "no thank you," when "yes" popped out. Suddenly, I was a school teacher.

It would be hard to describe the joy I received my first year, being paid to stand and share what I knew about natural science with a bunch of really good kids. The seventh graders were wide-eyed wonders, going through all the fun of transcending childhood for adulthood. That life science class was cool, and there were several really outstanding young biologists. The eighth graders were more into being teenagers, and their physical science class wasn't a huge motivator, unfortunately. Tenth grade was straight biology, but the administration wasn't too whoopie about my teaching evolution. They then busted a gasket when I answered all the students' questions about the human body – specifically the reproductive system. I think that's where we really fell out.

My ninth grade class was mine to create, so I threw together a low-level zoology class, complete with caged reptiles and amphibians, a preserved bird collection, and all kinds of other relics that turned my classroom into a proverbial museum. Some in the class really fell deep into zoology, and I know of three who are biologists today.

Two good kids in the class were Mark Baxley and Todd Goodson, and we became fast friends away from school as well. It wasn't long before we decided to head to Mexico that summer, for snakes, birds and Montezuma's revenge.

There were no earth-shattering stories from this trip, just a lot of tough birding in every corner of Mexico. I found myself surprised at the deforestation just since my previous trip, and wondered what the future held for this birding paradise. Still, I added several dozen life birds and showed Todd and Mark the time of their lives.

My absolutely favorite place was in Oaxaca, just up the mountain from the city of Oaxaca. There was (and still is in 2002) a protected cloud forest called Cerro San Felipe. Todd, Mark and I found a wonderful concentration of highland birds there, including wonderful little Dwarf Jays and stunning Red Warblers. This was my first experience with real cloud forests, and it just seemed like cheating to be in such a cool climate in the tropics, with all the tropical birds. Without the double-duty of snake hunting on this trip, we were able to get in much more montane birding, and many more life birds.

Upon my return, I decided to work in the public schools, so I accepted a position beginning an alternative school in Apalachicola, Florida. The kids were a trial, but afternoons were free to do field work, and I began a data base which was to be used as part of my eventual masters degree. I lived at Indian Pass, about halfway between Apalachicola and Cape San Blas. It was truly a birder's playground, and a fantastic place in the fall migration. I also ate more fresh fish and oysters, all harvested within a mile of my house, than any sane person can imagine.

After my second year, when my colleague Faith Whiteside and I had cut the county's dropout rate in half, we both decided to move on. With two years of migration data, I returned to graduate school that fall, and put an advanced degree after my name.

My third trip to Mexico was in January of 1983, with Jim Geil, my best friend from high school. I had just finished graduate school, and wanted to celebrate. Jim wasn't doing much of anything, and went along for the adventure. I wanted to see some West Mexican birds, and he wanted to see Acapulco, so it seemed like a convenient trip for both of us.

Yes, we saw my brother in Houston briefly, and roared down to Laredo in my (fairly) new truck. It had aged, as all my vehicles seem to do, prematurely. We cut diagonally across northern Mexico and eased our way down the west coast. There, I saw many great birds, such as Zone-tailed Hawk, White-throated Magpie-Jay, Elegant Quail, Purplish-backed Jay and Mountain Trogon. Actually, there were dozens of new species for me, as the west coast is quite different avifaunistically from the gulf lowlands.

I did have an interesting experience near Acapulco. I was birding in the hills, having just seen my first Solitary Eagle, and decided to cross this rocky river to bird the opposite side. Normally I have quite good balance, but I hopped on a very slippery rock, and absolutely busted my rear end in the river. I really hit hard, and wondered momentarily if I was injured. But what was so interesting, was the reaction of several kids playing along the bank. I looked at them, still a bit dazed, and not one of them saw anything funny about it (nor did I). I know that little band of snake hunters I brought to Mexico earlier would have busted their shorts laughing. I guess that's just a cultural thing.

We continued south all the way to Southern Mexico, where I added all kinds of tropical birds to my life list. There were not just rain forest species, the mountains of Chiapas and Oaxaca bore great fruit. Directions from my uncle's book helped immensely, allowing me to find natu-

White-throated Magpie-Jay ▶

ral areas where some of the tougher species could be found. As long as we kept moving, there were dozens of new birds everywhere, and my life list was exploding.

Arriving at the southern end of Mexico, we continued into Guatemala, and added some birds there as well. We did not find the Resplendent Quetzal, but the Lovely Cotinga just about melted my binoculars. The ratio of species to individuals in rain forests was amazing, where ten individuals may represent eight species. During this time, I learned to use the whole text identifying birds, such as the total length, the call notes, the habitat and certainly the geography. Figuring out unknown birds became an art form, and I dearly loved the challenge — and the new birds.

It was getting to be time to start north again, so we decided to return up the gulf slope. Jim was good about hanging out while I did my bird thing, which I have always appreciated. He would exact some measure of revenge, as I was to find out our last night in Mexico, though.

The morning of the fifteenth day, a few hundred miles from the Mexican border, we came upon an extensive marsh that teemed with birds, and no doubt snakes. I worked the marsh from the road (under the omnipresent watchful eyes of the Roadside Hawk), seeing tody-fly-catchers, crakes, an incredible Pinnated Bittern and loads of Northern Jacanas. However, there was a lot of thick stuff in the middle, and I knew there were new birds lurking in the island thicket. I had to have a look.

Changing from boots to sneakers, an act that probably saved my life, I eased out into the marsh. Below the surface it was pretty thick, so I had to part the water weeds with my hands to make any progress. The bottom was getting deeper as well, and it was frankly hard work getting out to the island. Nearly an hour later, I felt my feet find the bottom again, and I forced my tired frame up to the submerged bushes.

Rather than come out of the water, I eased myself all the way around the island's backside, checking out its inhabi-

Roadside Hawk ▼

tants. Four new birds blessed my morning swim, with a wren, a greenlet and two flycatchers, all tame and curious about this idiot invading their territory. Having circled the island, I started to split two smaller islands to beat a direct course back to the truck. With thick debris on both sides of me, my escape was suddenly cut off by a very beautiful snake. And a deadly one.

Right in front of me, lying on the surface, was a cantil, the aquatic pit viper with a bite of fire. Most snakes have an inherent fear of humans but this creature wasn't impressed. It just sat there as if to say, "You'll have to find another way out." You can bet this reptile had my full attention.

I don't kill snakes, although he tempted me to make an exception. I broke off a stick in a nearby bush, and prepared to do battle. I eased toward him to flick him out of the water, and to my amazement, he charged me! I should-n't have been so surprised, since I had very little experi-

Pinnated Bittern ▼

ence with Mexican snakes. It was time, though, to think fast.

I dug the end of the stick under his sleek body and was going to flip him out of the water, but the end caught in the water weeds, and broke. Wow, it was time for plan B. This guy was going to nail me right in the chest, as I was in five feet of water, and everything interesting about this turned very unfunny. In the split second I had, it seemed there was one possibility. As he came within a foot of me, I reached around behind him, grabbed his tail, and flung him rear end over tea kettle about thirty feet back in the tangles. Whew!

Wasting no time, I decided to cut straight across the marsh to shore, and call it a trip. Quickly, it got over my head, so I was dog paddling through the weeds. Leaving my binoculars in the truck seemed like the smartest thing I ever did. Going out there in the first place was clearly the dumbest. My feet continued to get tangled, I was really starting to suck air, and I found myself becoming totally exhausted. I was in a lot of trouble, and I knew drowning was not out of the question.

I debated calling Jim, but even if he could hear me, would he be any better off in this quagmire than I? Would I be condemning my best friend to the same fate? No, I got myself into this mess, and it was up to me to get out of it.

There were no tricks here, and it wasn't rocket science. I just called on every bit of strength I had, pulling forward with my hands, and trying to keep my feet untangled. Three times I rolled over on my back, went under, and raked off the long stems from around my feet. The third

time, I almost didn't come up. Giving up was a temptation, as I ached so badly I could hardly move. I honestly
believe that seeing a Turkey Vulture high overhead was my
greatest inspiration at the time, but I really just had to dig
deep and see what was there. It is at these times that we
find out what we are made of, and how easily we give up.

There was no turning point in this story, I just kept
making a tiny bit of progress across the marsh. I began
raking water weeds off my feet with the other foot, which
helped somewhat. I also tried more rapid breathing, like
athletes do when they are running. Once, I sucked up two
leaves from a plant, and that only managed to compound
my problems even more. But after about forty-five minutes, about thirty feet from shore, my right toe contacted
the bottom, and I was able to stand up on tip toes and
catch my lost breath. At that point, I knew I was going to
make it.

When I finally reached shore, I could hardly stand up,
and every muscle in my body ached. Jim probably thought
I was awfully selfish, taking a cool dip and not returning
as he waited patiently. He got some sense about my ordeal
when I returned to the truck and calmly said, "I want to
get out of Mexico, and I want to get out tonight."

I didn't bother to change as the breeze and wet clothes
cooled me down. I wasn't much into conversation, either,
and I think Jim knew it'd been a rough morning at the
marsh. Much thought went through my head about all the
life birds I had seen, and there was no way I could be anything but delighted about the trip. And being alive.

It was late January, but the weather was warm and the
wind blew out of the south harder and harder. Some dark

clouds passed over us, and they seemed to be heading south. Sure enough, it was a cold front passing over from the north, and the wind shifted quickly into our faces. Another act of nature became obvious, as I felt myself getting sick. The trauma of the morning, being wet all day, and the Mexican food, were all getting to me.

After supper, I tried to lie down in the back and sleep, with Jim driving. I nearly froze! Up to the front I came, and tried nodding off a bit. This was moderately successful, until Jim joined the party. He fell asleep at the wheel.

BAM! We took my new (getting old quick) truck into a guard rail on the left side, and it tore up the left front rather badly. Poor Jim. Honestly, I felt as sorry for him as I did for myself. He never does anything wrong. We were pretty well dead in the water, but not as much so as I nearly was that morning.

Using a crow bar to bend the fender and changing the ruined tire, we got moving, and made it to the Mexican border late that night. To say I was glad to be back in the states would be an understatement, and I looked forward to my warm bed. Jim shared the expenses of fixing my truck, and a vacation trip turned ugly was over. But I learned as much about traveling in third world countries as I did about birds.

Upon my return, I accepted a position teaching GED prep, pending a job more in my field. I spent the day helping high school dropouts learn enough to get their diploma, but found myself having misgivings about the worth of that document. It did give me some "down time" between students to dream about my next destination, and I decided on Costa Rica. I had an old buddy named

Wiley Clifford, a former participant in my camps, and we'd always talked about doing something crazy. So we agreed to fly to Costa Rica and hoof it for two weeks.

My all-important life list was now in the mid nine hundreds, and the thought of seeing five times this many species was as exciting as it seemed impossible. Still, it had been my goal since that dinner with Peterson, and I saw no reason to abandon it. I was also making fewer trips to the coast during the migration. I was growing a bit tired of the same old birds, and Cape May Warblers lost the excitement they'd once held. In retrospect, that was really sad.

Wiley and I flew down in June and immediately took a bus to famous Monte Verde. Here, there were lush montane rain forests, dark and deep. The first bird I saw on the trail was a Blue Dacnis [no.17], and I knew it was going to be a great trip. Several new tanagers were added to my list the first hour, and all kinds of neat tropical groups came into focus during the course of that day.

Late morning, we experienced one of the great ornithological finds in the world. A male Respendent Quetzal made his appearance, and the beauty was simply staggering. The metallic colors, the long, flowing tail coverts and the regal look truly made this the king of western birds. Once again, I convinced myself that one life bird wasn't necessarily as good as another.

Our short visit to Volcan Rincon was pleasant enough, but the black flies worked over our elbows very professionally. The entire time in Costa Rica, we had welts from this part of the trip, and the itch was nearly unbearable. We were told they were here on account of the cows, which makes a good argument for staying away from pastures. We did see a lot of new birds at this beautiful place, but I will never forget our consternation and subsequent surprise over one identification.

It seems there were these small hummingbirds flying everywhere. Were they coquettes? Possibly another small species, such as the Bee Hummingbird, the smallest bird in the world? They seemed to have a tail band, but nothing in the guide satisfied our thirst for an identity. As our frustrations came to a climax, we finally realized sheepishly that we were looking at sphinx moths!

Wiley and I caught the bus up to Santa Rosa National Park and thoroughly enjoyed a few days in the dry forest near Nicaragua. It was great having monkeys in the canopy, and they were so effervescent! The dry forest, as you may know, was disappearing rapidly, until we discovered that large ungulates such as cows help spread the trees' seeds, mimicking the large mammals of ice ages gone by.

We took a day and hiked all the way out to the Pacific beach, and that was one of the most memorable days of my life. The birding was excellent along the way, with all sorts of finches flitting up from the trail, and forest birds in the canopy. The lowland forest became my first experience with the exquisite land crabs, those big fellows which are absolutely red. Not long after that we began hearing a roar in the distance, and with little experience, wondered what it was (not the ever-present Howler Monkeys). It grew louder and louder, until we crossed a salt lagoon, burst over extraordinarily high dunes, and saw the mighty Pacific Ocean in all its splendor.

This was a real treat, as waves were pounding so hard it shook the earth beneath our feet. We were in somewhat of a cove, with great cliffs jutting out several hundred yards in either direction. There were also birds flying low over the water, always right to left, which I quickly identified as Brown Boobies, one of my most wanted life birds. Speaking of that species, there were several very attractive ladies soaking up more sun than usual down on the beach.

Wiley and I relaxed and birded around this impressive area for part of the afternoon, but knew we had to return before dark. In the tropics, days are seldom more than twelve hours, so the warm days of summer seem all-too-short. It had been a triumphant morning, to say the least, but there was no way I could have known what the afternoon had in store.

We had walked about an hour toward camp, through the Canyon del Tigre, stopping at several places to simply halt and look into the canopy for birds. There were many fruit-eaters around, such as parrots, trogons, toucans and all the rest. In one place though, as we stood still, I glanced up the trail in utter disbelief. In all my years of traveling the world, this may rank as my most surprised moment.

A huge male Jaguar ambled across the trail right out in front of God and everybody. It was like being a prisoner in time and space. I was but a spectator in this great cat's life. Even though I viewed him but for a moment or two, I remember to this day details about him that will stand etched in my mind forever. His muscles rippled up and down his stout legs. His mouth was partially open, like he was hot and looking for shade. The end of his tail flicked slightly as he stepped across the middle of the trail. I was in the presence of some ethereal greatness, the god of the jungle. Yet, at no point was I the least bit scared, here in the Tigre's canyon. I was simply in total awe.

The rest of the stay at Santa Rosa was very pleasant, though hardly as exciting as the few moments of feline fantasy. I enjoyed watching the groundskeepers "mowing" the grass with their machetes, by bending over low to the ground and whacking back and forth. Some of the primates were tame and abiding, and various frugivorous birds added color and excitement to camp.

We decided it was time to head for the southern part of the country, as our days were half over. We spent some time in the high country south of San Jose, and loved the cloud forest right along the highway. Three birds stick in my mind as being real favorites here. The Long-tailed Silky-Flycatchers were absolutely breathtaking, as they sailed out over the edge, train in tow, looking like so many airborne fairies. For sheer gaudiness, the Flame-throated Warblers started where Yellow-throated Warblers leave off, with their fiery-orange throats nearly catching the canopy aflame. Still, my favorite bird was the modest little Timberline Wren, marooned in its unique niche, far from its fellow troglodytes. I so love high mountain birds!

Our destination was the unparalleled tropical ornithologist, Dr. Alexander Skutch. Author of untold numbers of avian and ecological articles and books, he was one of my true heroes. Directions told us to take one certain bus into the hills from a small town, and ask the locals where he lived. We were arriving sight unseen, and knew he may just throw us clean off his land, but that was a chance we were more than willing to take.

We boarded a rather warm bus, and found a seat with a mom and three small children in front of us, and an old man behind us. Off we went, smoke billowing into the air, and potholes that could swallow tyrannosaurs. It was an uncomfortable ride, but we humored ourselves by bird watching out the window.

"Wiley, there's a Turquoise-browed Motmot [no.28]." Good-natured Wiley nodded agreeably and went back into thought.

"Those are oropendalas out there; doncha see the white spot on the head and the yellow in the tail?" Again, Wiley smiled and returned to his thoughts.

"I think those were Smooth-billed Anis, Wiley." My good friend was about to patronize me one more time when the old man leaned over the seat from behind and said, "Actually, those were groove-bills. They have a lower ridge on the bill. We don't get many smooth-bills up here."

As I sat quietly having a corvid lunch, the man asked us where we were going. Fearing the worst, I replied we were wanting to meet Dr. Skutch. Sure enough, he quietly asked, "How was it?" I just hate it when other people are funny — especially at my expense.

Wiley and I looked at each other like our hair was on fire and turned to make friends with a legend. Dr. Skutch invited us to his farm to stay in his spare building, and dine with him and his very British wife. They took us in like we were family and showed us every hospitality. They were simply charming people, and I especially liked his wit, such as when he referred to his horse as the lawn mower.

The next morning, Wiley and I were treated to a field trip around Dr. Skutch's property. In a way, I realized how valuable it was for me to know the calls of North American birds, because we had been so stumped by many calls in Costa Rica until the master identified them for us. We saw an incredible variety of birds for such a small area, and the fact that they feel unthreatened by humans, and are tame, cannot be overstated.

The "bird of the day" for Wiley and me was the bellbird. We were just walking along being fairly quiet, soaking up Dr. Skutch's wisdom, when we heard this unceremonious BONG! I had wondered when I'd hear a bellbird, but it was my first, so it didn't dawn on me what it was. Dr. Skutch calmly identified the sound, but we were a tad more than calm. Bellbirds are notoriously hard to see in their canopy home, but finally we saw this handsome creature, who quickly became far more than a tick on my life list. I'll never forget those three wattles hanging loosely over his bill, giving him his name (Three-wattled Bellbird).

It has never been so hard leaving a place as this tropical farm, but time was running short. We took the bus farther south, and found a wooded stream leading up a mountainside. Here we camped, and decided this would be our last birding spot before returning back to central Costa Rica.

That night, I tallied my all-important life list and found myself four short of a thousand life birds.

I must get these tomorrow, because I just can't wait any longer. Frankly, I didn't enjoy the inner pressure it caused, but I was driven by the image of Dr. Peterson, and the promise I had made to myself. Sleep did not come easy, either, thanks to the uncertainty of tomorrow's birds.

Morning found me wide awake, wondering when it would be light enough to see birds. Finally, we stirred and had a few bites of granola. We didn't take any water, as this was before the time that our species couldn't walk across the hall of our office complex without a bottle of water in our hands. I acted like it was just another day, but my life list was very much at the forefront of my thoughts.

Almost immediately, we found a small insectivorous flock organizing in the lower canopy. There was the oddest flycatcher, with a monster bill and an orangish crown. My fingers poured over the pages in short order, as they had learned to do, and though I knew this bird was a *Platyrinchus*, it was now apparent that it was indeed a Golden-crowned Spadebill. I wondered how they called that golden.

One of my nemesis birds had always been the Green Shrike-Vireo. As we stepped off the trail and looked over a forest clearing, this handsome creature stared at us as if to say, "If you were smaller, I'd have you for breakfast." Ooops, better make sure it's not a Yellow-browed Shrike-Vireo. Yup. Well, two down and two to go.

We came to a wide part of the stream around midmorning, and a very striking bird caught my eye. I wasn't sure what it was, but I knew I'd never seen one. The huge light patch at the base of the tail made this one a cinch, especially when I vaguely remembered it from the field guide. There it is — a Buff-rumped Warbler! It was wagging its tail hither and yon, as active as waterthrushes and Spotted Sandpipers. Biology is as beautiful as life birds.

Gulp. That brings me to 999. It looked like a certainty that I would pass a thousand; the question was, which bird would get that honor? A tanager? Likely. A warbler? That would be nice. Maybe something regal like a hawk. Not a good place for birds of prey. What then?

It wasn't a lingering question, for in no more than two minutes, a large bird flew up from the marshy edge at the end of an opening, and perched right out on a bare branch for easy viewing. Obviously a wader, it was clearly an adult Bare-throated Tiger-Heron. Oh, man. The fine barring on the neck was such a treat, and this bird, though I never would have guessed this species, was a perfect way to reach my magic goal.

Today, I have seen dozens of Bare-throated Tiger-Herons, and they always remind me of a nervous morning in Costa Rica, when numbers seem to matter. For the record, though, I saw eleven more life birds that day, and felt a little silly for worrying. Inwardly I quietly celebrat-

ed being one-fifth the way to my goal, and central Costa Rica could get me well on my way to another thousand.

The two slopes of this central-mountain country are loaded with birds! The Pacific side is blessed with a wonderful area called Carara, near the coastal town of Tarcoles, where the lowland jungle was replete with antbirds such as Dusky and Chestnut-backed Antbirds, Black-hooded Antshrike, Dot-winged Antwren, Black-faced Antthrush and a marvelous Streak-chested Antpitta. This was only the beginning of the forest birds, but it opened up a whole new love of mine. Antbirds will always be the exciting glue that holds tropical rain forest walks together, and their secretive natures and challenging identifications truly make them the special creatures they are.

There were all kinds of other groups around as well, including toucans, two trogons, several parrots, a few tough flycatchers and lowland tanagers. I enjoyed poking around in the mangroves of Tarcoles for mangrove endemics, and the brilliant Scarlet Macaws that lit up the atmosphere with both color and thunderous calls.

From the hideous caldera of Poas Volcano down the Carribean slope, there was a whole 'nother set of tropical birds. The group that dominated these three days were hummingbirds, from the Purple-throated Mountain-gems [no.30]and Magnificent Hummingbirds of the highlands to the hermits, thorntails, emeralds, and many other groups at mid-elevations. These allowed me to add over a hundred lifers since my tiger-heron, and I was able to leave Costa Rica feeling that 2000 wasn't quite as far away.

◀ Bare-throated Tiger Heron

I also really enjoyed Wiley's company, and his friendship to this day. Those who share the beauty and interest of nature have a special bond that transcends the trials of the day.

CHAPTER FOUR

TROUBLES AND TRIUMPHS IN SOUTH AMERICA

COLOMBIA

In the fall of 1983 I accepted a teaching position at Leon High School, my Alma Mater. It was a little like "Welcome Back Cotter," with a few teachers finding it hard to believe that an uninspired student from the 70's could return as a teacher in the 80's. This was more than a job, though, as I literally loved this grand old place with my whole heart. I quickly rose to teaching the honors and gifted students, and they inspired me to no end.

In all my years teaching at Leon, I only missed one day legitimately sick. But when a really good fall or spring cold front blew through, I called in sick and headed for St. George Island birding. On my leave form I always put "barometric flu" for the infirmity, and the assistant principal knew where I was and what I was doing. Being the decent person that he was, he realized that these trips were making me a better science teacher.

I tried hanging around in Florida that first summer, but never made it. I left in July with two students— Scott Schnitzer and Jeff Madsen — for Yucatan and Guatemala. We visited Tikal National Park, and the birding was excellent, as it was at Palenque. Still, I noticed that I was having to work harder and harder for life birds, as my experience in Central America grew. I only added 36 life birds, and vowed it was time for a change.

My second year at Leon I quietly dreamed of South America, and it occupied more than a small part of my consciousness. I began pouring over books, and discovered Peter Alden's book on finding birds around the world. This was to be my first really great trip, which, I suppose, means one outside of my continent. I saved up every penny, often eating peanut butter and jelly sandwiches for supper, and by June had $3,400 for my travels.

On June 6, 1985, I took a step which would really put me on the road toward 5000 bird species. I boarded an American Airlines bound for Cali, Columbia, and sat in coach wondering if I had any idea what I was doing. When I stepped off the plane on a steamy runway, my false ego triumphantly shook my fist in the air, but inwardly I was feeling a bit insecure. I rented a clinker to drive, and wandered out of the city toward the famous Old Cali/St. Bonaventure Road. There I spent a cramped night writing in my journal and boning up on Colombian birds. I was tempted to delve into the delicious brownies a friend sent with me, but held off for a more special occasion.

The first few pages of my journal I quoted Jonathan Swift, where he said, "May you live all the days of your life." I also dealt with the very real possibility that I may not return from this trip, but wrote that I had lived more in 32 years than many folks do in a lifetime. I supposed all this thought of death emanated from the cautions and warnings my family and friends threw my way upon leaving, so thanks a lot! But with the rain pounding on top of my small car, not knowing exactly where I was, hungry, and exhausted, I could have felt better about things. So, I just went to sleep.

There are no words in my language to describe the day that was to come! Fantastic. Monumental. Unbelievable. I saw no less than 82 new birds for my life list, and my heart just raced all day. The vivid colors in the tropical birds became permanently etched on my brain, and the diversity of tanagers simply blew my mind. I spent several hours by flashlight in my tent that second night — camped by a clear stream — pouring over identifications of difficult birds. I couldn't have gone to sleep anyway; I was so excited! Tallahassee, Leon, family and friends seemed insignificantly distant, and all I wanted to do was have days like this the rest of my life. It was my first day in South America, and my life list was already over 1200!

Over the next few days, I worked the little trio of Andean mountain ranges in Colombia, and added so many new birds I could hardly keep up. My favorite bird was the Long-tailed Tyrant, a solid black flycatcher with a long tail and a white cap. But there were so many handsome, sensational and colorful birds, it was hard to choose. Antbirds, toucans, handsome flycatchers, diverse hummers, metallic trogons, beautiful grosbeaks and an incredible assortment of tanagers. I took their picture with my little binocam, a set of binoculars with a 110mm lens built in. Haven't you ever seen a bird through your binoculars, and just wanted to hit a button and take its picture? Well, thanks to Barney Parker, one of several mentors I was lucky enough to have, I clicked on bird after bird all through the Andes.

There were certainly lots of serpents as well. Of the first 14 snakes I saw, each represented a different species. Talk about diversity. It was the fifteenth that would threaten my life, but also bring me great joy and fulfillment. That would come in a few days, with some great birding between here and there.

I stayed in Popayan, and headed to Parque de Munchique and the paramo of Parque de Purace for excellent high mountain birding. I was hoping to see Andean Condors in Purace, but the foggy weather conditions prohibited that. This great vulture was one of five "most wanted" species I'd chosen for my South American trip. The other four were an albatross, penguin, skua and cock of the rock. Despite being shut out of these five "target birds," the life birds were piling up at an amazing rate. My favorites from Purace were Andean Teal, Black-chested Buzzard-Eagle and Red-throated Caracara [no.2].

Because of the pleasant temperatures, I tended to bird mountains more than lowlands, but I knew this had to change. Therefore, I selected a small town called Milan as my next destination. It was down on Amazonas, hot and muggy. The road there was increasingly bad as I neared Milan, but the birding was great. The raptors were tame

Black-chested Buzzard-Eagle ▶

and the assortment of flycatchers dizzying. Finally, I got to one last hill before Milan, and it was nearly straight down. I rode the brakes all the way down, and dust billowed up around me and into the open windows. I remember smiling and wondering what that road would have been like wet. Be careful what you wonder.

I checked into a $2/night hotel and read as much as I could about lowland birds. Also, there's my journal to catch up on, as things have been pretty hectic. I've skipped much about the car trouble encountered with this (ab)used rental car, but suffice to say, not all my time has been spent birding or driving.

The next morning came early, and I was headed down the river by dawn. It was pleasant at that hour, but heat and humidity would follow. Slowly picking my way through the riparian forest and cleared fields, new bird after new bird popped up. My favorite of the day was the

Hoatzin, rather like a reptile with feathers. They are large, hissing birds with huge crests and flagrant reddish plumage. They flop around in the trees along the river, eating leaves when the stomach beckons. Their young have claws on their wings for clambering around on limbs, making them appear like some relic of an eon gone by.

Equally exciting was a Sunbittern, which nearly defies description. It is a large "wading" bird that spends most of its time skulking on banks and limbs, flashing its rather incredible and unlikely wing patterns as a flash color for defense. Its whistled song always seems to be the same four notes (I have perfect pitch): an A, B-flat, F and E. The first two are slurred, followed by two counts, then the final two notes are somewhat marcato. Curiously, I have heard them make completely different calls in Venezuela on later trips.

The hours slipped by as new birds blessed my day. Coming back I circled around and hit a few patches of for-

est missed earlier. Hearing a commotion, though, I eased over to the great river, and suddenly found out the object of the birds' scorn. There before me, at the bottom of an embankment, coiled the largest snake I've ever seen. It was absolutely monstrous — over fourteen feet — and as big around as my leg. It was basically shiny brown with dark spots, and had a huge head. It was the snake I'd dreamed of catching since my earliest days watching Wild Kingdom, with that nutcase (also named Jim) who jumped out of trucks and boats to wrestle the mightiest creatures on earth.

As you may have guessed, it was an anaconda. For several minutes, I was captured by the splendor of this gargantuan reptile. The muscles rising above its spine swelled with each breath, its thick neck led to its massive head with iridescence, and inside its huge gape were the largest teeth of any nonpoisonous snake on earth. That serpent was quite a load!

I had to have it. Clearly, the snake was adept at escaping enemies (the few there were) by sliding off into the river, where it would be king of its domain. It would be necessary to grab it before it made its plunge, as it could pull me under if its tail secured a purchase on any underwater log. I wasn't scared, crazy or impulsive. I just knew this was something I had to do, for all the dreams I'd had of this moment. I slowly backed away from the bank, placed my back pack and optics on soft grass, and gulped heavily.

With a war whoop like a Klingon, I ran toward the edge and sailed out into the space overlooking the great snake. The plan was to land beside him, secure his head, and drag him up the bank. The reality was that I landed five feet up the bank, my boots slipped out from under me a la banana peel, and I went tumbling you-know-what over tea kettle past this astonished creature. My spontaneous amendment to plan A was that I grabbed this reptilian monstrosity as I slid past, and the both of us rolled unceremoniously into the muddy alluvium. Ker-SPLASH!

For a split second I thought about trying to find his head just before we hit the water, but he was kind enough to show it to me – deep into my left shoulder. Oh, man. Even with arms, coils and legs flying everywhere, the intense pain of 42 centimeter-long needles into my flesh screamed for attention. I grabbed the monster's head and pried it off my shoulder, already bleeding like a stuck pig. Then, for several minutes, slipping and sliding on the clay bank, I tried to work this unmanageable leviathan out of the water. At least I now understood their scientific name, which means "that which bites quickly."

There is little doubt in my mind that had there been an underwater stump for him to wrap his tail around, I would have died, wet and very alone. The same would also probably be true had he not been cold blooded and we mammals warm blooded. But eventually, my stamina wore out this beast, and within twenty minutes I sat at the top of the bank, with blood still staining my white shirt, and both hands holding the scaley devil's head. I was exhausted, totally gross, and in as much pain as I've ever felt, but I was on top of the earth!

In about a half-hour, I was joined by many of the townspeople, and I shared with them about anacondas as much as my horrendous Spanish could tell. The main point was that although it would bite (that would have been a hard secret to keep), it was nonpoisonous. Somehow they believed anacondas ate fish, and were then the enemy, competing with their fishing poles. We straightened that out. And they were sure this beast would have eaten one of their children, but I assured them it was more afraid of them than they were of it. I was not altogether sure of that.

At the end of the demonstration, many were disappointed to find out this huge snake was not for dinner. In one heave, I sent the snake sliding down the now-muddy embankment, and he disappeared into the brown abyss. Several in the group appreciated what I had shared, and others just seemed to accept that this gringo was completely mad. But I also sensed a deep hostility among some, and it would become more apparent as the night wore on.

I dragged my worn out self back into Milan and had my favorite – arroz con pollo (chicken and rice) – before spending the balance of the afternoon sitting under the shade of a large fruiting tree with the field guide. My shoulder was really in pain, but after a good scrubbing with soap, it didn't figure to be a problem, and wasn't.

That evening, though, the problems came. Slowly at first, and then reaching almost a fevered pitch, some in the town walked the streets shouting slogans which were directed either at me, Americans in general, or maybe all foreigners. I think they'd been listening to Radio Cuba. There were objects like rocks thrown in my direction, and the "protestors" gathered right outside my room. I thought how ironic it would be if I survived wrestling a monstrous anaconda, only to be beaten to death by an angry mob.

I tried to study the field guide and ignore the ruckus outside when a huge, thundering sound shook my small residence. Startled at first, I then smiled as I realized it was, in fact, thunder. And plenty of lightning. Finally, the skies opened up and it just poured. I mean torrentially. The last thing I heard was the pitter patter of feet racing for shelter. That's also the last thing I remembered, as for the only time in my life, I fell asleep with the light on. And man, did I sleep!

I decided to leave early the next morning, without breakfast or any goodbyes. The hotel people wouldn't take my money because they were embarrassed by the behavior of the townspeople, though the few dollars meant very little to me. As I packed up my car, I assumed I'd be gone in mere minutes, but nature had other ideas.

Driving out the east side of town, I came to the hill from hell, and realized it was totally inundated by the long, driving rain. Just walking up it brought squishy noises and very muddy feet. Truthfully, it reminded me of Cheryl and me attempting Attigan Pass in Northern Alaska, with its pea-soup constitution. This actually might have been worse, as much of it was red clay. Oh, man.

Glancing in the opposite direction, I noticed a soccer field stretching for a hundred yards or so, which pretty well was a straight shot to the hill. I backed up as far as I could into the far "end zone" and took off like a scalded dog. I truly believe the front wheels left the ground when I smashed into the bottom of the steep incline, and my back snapped with the sudden forward motion. What a surprise, I wasn't wearing my seat belt.

Mud flew in every direction, and the engine raced with reckless abandon. I had to throw on the wipers as the windshield turned reddish brown, and my side pane was hopelessly painted with wet earth. Amazingly, I made it near the top, slowing to a stop, when the car seemed to gain traction. It lurched forward as if magically pushed, and actually seemed to get stronger as I neared the level road over the incline. Then I realized it wasn't magically pushed; it was Hispanically pushed!

About a half-dozen guys saw what was going on and ran to help. They were covered with mud but having the time of their lives. You'd think they just scored the winning goal in the World Cup. Being about as grateful as I've ever been, I pulled myself out of the front seat and shook each muddy hand. They wouldn't take money for their help, and I suspect they were also feeling bad about the night before. But then it hit me; I had just the thing.

I pulled out the package of homemade brownies I'd been hoarding and we all sat and ate like hogs. There was laughter, good fellowship, and friendships made. I got in a few last thoughts about the beneficiality of snakes, and they each shared how they liked norteamericanos. It was with a heavy heart that I finally put my aching body back in the car and eased on down the road. Recuerdos a todos!

It was a long, rough drive to Garzon, but there were several opportunities to see neat birds in stops with various habitats. I had learned long ago that to maximize my bird listing time, I should visit every available habitat. This I did, and added nine lifers on what was basically a travel day. Late in the day, though, trouble visited again, as the trip seemed to constantly take on highs and lows.

I picked up a hitchhiker who really stole my heart. He tried hard to speak English, he seemed interested in the birds in my field guide, and then stole my heart when he offered for me to stay at his little house. Then, when I stopped for a coke, and he walked away toward his home, he stole my wallet. This I didn't even realize until I was 12 miles down the road and low on gas, with no moola.

This was too much, and I just felt sick. I could stay in town to try to get money the next day at the bank, but so much was in my wallet! I had no cash, the banks were closed for the day, there was little gas left, and I had a huge decision to make. But I felt more anger than anything, so I turned around and headed back to find that little twerp.

Playing detective for a little while, I found out where this guy was, all alone in his hut. Having far more testosterone than brains at the moment, I blasted through the door and confronted Miguel inches from his face. Standing nearly a foot taller than him, I offered to trade him his life for my wallet; a deal he couldn't refuse. Seeing that virtually all the money was there, I immediately left and headed toward Cali. I have often found pause to regret my rage that day, being a nonviolent person, but sometimes things just pile up to where we cannot control our anger. You'll just have to believe that I was at the end.

ECUADOR

Colombia had been quite the introduction to South

America. There had been inescapable beauty, an incredible diversity of birds, hassles that could make your hair fall out, and the neatest snakes imaginable. Mostly, though, it was adventure from stem to stern. Now I had arrived via bus in Ecuador, and this would be a cake walk. Right? We'll see.

Quito was a lovely little city set in the Andes, with a lot more excitement than oxygen. Natives were everywhere, selling their wares and bidding this supposedly rich gringo a good morning. It was hard not to like this place, and there seemed to be a kinder spirit here than in much of Colombia. Renting a car was neither hard nor expensive, and soon I was on my way up famed Mt. Coatapoxi.

There was no shortage of life birds up the winding road, but the view at the treeless puna zone was breathtaking, from scenic beauty as well as oxygen depredation. My favorite bird was the Carunculated Caracara, but the wild mustangs left behind by the Spanish Conquistadors really stole the show. Neat waterbirds were everywhere, with the Andean Lapwings quite striking. I even tried the hike up the snow to look for something new and exciting, and it felt like my lungs would burst. Still, being in the snow on the equator was an amazing experience, birds or no birds.

My next day in Ecuador was equally memorable, as I worked the road from Nono to Mindo. The canopy from huge trees down the mountain stretched up to eye level, allowing me to look squarely into the birds' homes. From the first aracari to the last yellowish tanager, it was a day full of mountain birds. I added several dozen life birds on this bonanza day, and had one of the more pleasant days birding ever in the field.

There were several more great days around Quito, although each seemed to yield fewer and fewer life birds (as would be expected). Soon, it was time to head downslope to Amazonas, as the birdlife in the lower mountains was equally exciting. With altitudinal ecology, each elevation has its own characteristic species, and a long walk down a steep road could pass through several life zones in a morning. I didn't stay long at the bottom, as the birds were rather similar to those I found around Milan, Colombia. Besides, I had big plans I was only whispering to myself about.

Once back in Quito, I headed down the western slope to Guayaquil, a singularly rough city on the Pacific coast. I spent two days birding these warm lowlands, enjoying the antshrikes, Snail Kites and gnatwrens. It wasn't a great diversity, being dry lowland, but it certainly plugged some

holes in my list, and brought me to over 1400 species. I also did some checking around, as the biologist in me wouldn't let go of the dream to visit the land of Darwin's finches and big reptiles.

At last, around noon, I had a lead. I found out I could gain a ride on a cargo vessel named the Iguana, all the way out to the Galapagos. I'll spare you the details, as the whole arrangement wasn't exactly on the up-and-up. Oh, man. I was so excited I went to a restaurant and just gorged myself, as my meals hadn't been too whoopie for many days. I totally pigged out, and was equally worn out by the schedule I'd been keeping. As the boat left early in the morning, I decided to get a decent room and crash with my field guide the rest of the afternoon.

You have no idea how sick you can get, until Montezuma really nails you after a big meal. By late afternoon, my anterior and posterior were having a contest. It was the most violently sick I have ever been, and I was literally delirious for several hours. Where these microbes came from, I didn't know, but they were playing nature's Drano all through my system. Never have I felt so sorry for myself.

Sometime in the wee hours of the morning I fell asleep, and the wake-up knock on my door came awfully early. I was almost too weak to answer, and seriously considered lying back down and crashing. Do the mature thing. Yup, I'd take care of my body, and ensure some better health. Play it safe and sleep some more.

Yeah, right. I sprang up out of bed like a bolt, and nearly fainted from all the forces of evil that had worked so professionally on me the past 16 hours. I showered, which

◀ *Andean Lapwing*

I badly needed, threw together my belongings, and headed out the door within twenty minutes of being awakened. I picked up some cheap pastry, always available on street corners, and headed down to the dock. Within minutes, I had my little "place" on the boat and I had to pinch myself that this wasn't the same dream I'd had for years about going to the magical place of Darwinian origins.

About an hour later the Iguana steamed out of port and allowed me to pick up several new sea birds as we left sight of the mainland. The sun came out and I lay down and fell into the deepest sleep imaginable. For several hours I was totally wiped from consciousness, and slowly opened my eyes as we bounced along the Humboldt Current. As I stared obliquely across the turbulent waves, there was a form sailing across the waters that had me pinching myself again.

It was an albatross! My first-ever albatross! The species was the Waved Albatross of the Galapagos Islands, a portent of things to come. There were other pelagic birds out over the rough seas (and really cool flying fish as well), but to finally see an albatross nearly made me catatonic. It would sail along without flapping its wings, and then turn on a dime with one wing tip down and the other straight up. It wasn't as large as the albatross I'd one day see in the southern oceans, but it looked pretty good at that moment.

Our first stop was San Christobal, where we would dock for nearly two days. The walk through town was remarkable, with several species of Darwin's finches hopping around everywhere. I worked hard on their identifications, but realized early on that I'd not be able to sort out every one of them. In time, though, they became easier. One branch of them, which I called the tree finch branch, had the three species of tree finches, plus the two tool users (Mangrove and Woodpecker finches), and the interesting Vegetarian Finch (a little left-wing bird that thinks the carnivores are savages). The other large branch had the four ground finches, plus the two cactus finches. The curious Warbler Finch seemed less related to these more traditional species.

The walk up the hillside also produced other Galapagos endemics, such as the Galapagos Hawk [no.40], Large-billed Flycatcher and Galapagos Mockingbird (plus an honest-to-goodness Short-eared Owl!). There were also neat waterbirds along the shore, such as Lava Herons, Lava Gulls and various boobies. But the birds I really wanted to see were the Great Frigatebird, and the Swallow-tailed Gull [no.38].

My book said there was a colony of this species on the northeast corner of San Cristobal, but the warden told me they weren't there. It was a tough call, but I decided I believed the book. Bright and early the next morning, I struck out around the island's east shore for the destination I'd chosen, and I walked until well after noon before reaching an obvious colony. Indeed, they were Great Frigatebirds! The males had a green sheen, the females had white chins, and they all had light bars across their wings. I took some pictures, ate several granola bars, and headed back.

It became quickly obvious that I'd be back well after dark, so brainless here decided to walk over the top of the island and cut the corner. Unfortunately, every sticker, thorn and rough limb on the island attacked my bare legs and I returned around 9pm in pretty bad shape. My legs were bleeding, I was a combination of dehydrated and starving, and I was feeling like an idiot for not following the shoreline. But hey, lesson learned.

The next day it was on to Santa Cruz, home of the Charles Darwin Research Station. I enjoyed visiting with those people, and just imagining what history was made by their name sake, right here on these tiny little islands. Wandering around looking at creatures such as the Marine and Land iguanas, various mockingbirds and of course, the finches, just made this biology teacher full of wonder. This was like the epicenter of biology, as far as I was concerned.

There are several outstanding birds and other animals on the Galapagos, including the sea lions and requiem sharks that chase each other around, the big Galapagos Hawk, the cute little Sally Lightfoot Crabs, and the breathtaking tropicbirds that seemed like nature's best example of grace and elegance. But above all, the second of my "five most wanted list" came my way underwater, as a Galapagos Penguin swam right by me while snorkeling on a coral reef.

One day I hired a boat to take me to one of the breeding colonies of sea birds, and it was certainly a rich experience. Just like the finches and other land birds, these marvelous creatures had no fear of me, though I kept some distance from them out of respect. Waved Albatross, tropicbirds and boobies were all just sitting around incubating, not paying me the slightest attention. Thank goodness for the money ecotourism brings to places such as the Galapagos, to ensure these kinds of treasures are preserved for posterity.

It was hard to leave nature's laboratory, but it doesn't take long to find and identify just about all the Galapagos species. It was time to return to the mainland, and on to yet another country.

PERU

My health was less than ideal at this point of the trip, reminding me of the infirmity that plagued Darwin the rest of his life, following his voyage to South America on the Beagle. Subsequent to my horrible night in Guayaquil, and some shots a doctor administered, my bowels didn't move for a week (!), and I was quite weak. Despite this rather embarrassing condition, I began losing weight rapidly, and only my enthusiasm for nature kept me going at such a furious clip. Therefore, when I returned to Guayaquil, I hopped a bus and headed for Lima, Peru.

The drive down northern Peru was interesting. The climate calls for fog almost everyday, spawned by the close proximity to the cool Humboldt Current, spilling out of the Antarctic. Often it doesn't rain for years, but the fog allows for some vegetational growth. The homes are made of dried mud, presumably with the help of the nearby ocean. However, every few years, when the rains return briefly, these mud dwellings often disintegrate or become otherwise unlivable.

Once there, I rented a VW from a very lovely agent in the airport, for a mere $20/week. Wishing to get out of the singularly unattractive city of Lima, I stopped just long enough to flush a toilet, just to see the water swirl in the opposite direction. Besides, I hadn't flushed many toilets lately.

The drive down to Paracas got interesting very quickly. My favorite bird was the Red Shoveler, but there were all kinds of beautiful waterfowl, hawks and seabirds out over the water. Proverbial clouds of Peruvian Boobies and Pelicans crashed into the water like miniature bombs, with Inca Terns flitting over the surface like so many butterflies. They hovered over the top of feeding seals, and then snapped up minnows as the mammals rose to the surface. An uncommonly beautiful bird, these terns have forsaken the typical whitish plumage for dark, striking colors and patterns. The pelicans were similar enough to the Browns of my youth, except they were absolutely huge!

At one point I had worked up quite a thirst, as well as trying to force myself to eat, so I dropped into a small restaurant nestled between the highway and the Pacific coastline. The fresh fish I ordered was excellent, a testament to the bounty of life offered by the productive, cold waters of the Humboldt Current. However, the only cold drink they had was Polar Beer, and my personal policy is to never support the alcohol industry. Reluctantly, I ordered a cold one, and it tasted a little like dishwater. I wasn't alone in this opinion, as I eased out the door and poured the balance on a sensitive plant. Like an offended anemone, that poor little shrub closed up till a week from Friday.

Paracas was everything it was advertised to be. Cheap trips out of the harbor take ecotourists to see a plethora of sea birds, plus marine mammals (which are far more endearing to most than me). The day was pleasant enough, with no real surprises, until a skua roared past, making life miserable for a Kelp Gull. This guided missile, one of my five "target birds," stayed around and played harbor patrol most of the day, and offered great looks at a bird I'd only dreamed of seeing my entire life.

From Paracas, it was time to make one of the toughest drives I have ever attempted. I cut across the high puna zone toward Cuzco, which was several hundred miles of rough terrain. The highlight of the trip was the salt flats at Salinas, with more than 20,000 flamingos of no less than four species, including Greater Flamingo [no.29]. There were also many other interesting waterbirds. This was an adventurous day, but it got a little more hairy than I wanted at one point.

Somewhere near Ayacucho, while I was driving along checking out the Red-backed Hawks, I heard a sound that resembled the crackling of distant gunfire. I had been warned that this area wasn't the safest location on earth, and suddenly my attention was drawn to first and last

◀ Peruvian Boobies and Pelicans

things. I heard another noise and looked up to see two bullet holes in the roof of my car! My god, I was being shot at!

Needless to say, I put the pedal to the metal and sped off as fast as my little doodlebug would carry me. That was one unnerving experience, and made it hard to concentrate on birds the rest of the day. Very late in the afternoon, I pulled into a small town for gasoline, absolutely running on fumes. My tank was filled by scooping out one gallon at a time from an oil drum, and pouring it into my tank. The next morning, after a very cold night camping, I took off for Cuzco without incident.

The touristy city of Cuzco, famous for its proximity to Machu Picchu, is nestled in the mountains at about 12,000 feet. To reach the grandmother of all ruins, one must drive north to Urabamba and take a train to Machu Picchu. This I did, and must admit, the place is astonishing. The view off the top is splendid, and the forest along the road is replete with birds.

Better for birds, though, is the railroad tracks heading north. There were many seed-eating birds along the grassy sides of the tracks, and good forest birding at the edge of the woods. It was at one such spot, by a fruiting tree, that my ornithological cup overflowed. My attention was grabbed by a hefty perching bird, about the size of a small crow, but brownish. Then, with binoculars up, the most amazing creature flew into my field of view, by the female I had been watching. It was a male Andean Cock-of-the-Rock! His Majesty just sat there and radiated red all through the canopy. Oh, then he stepped into the sun! What an incredibly beautiful creature!

1. *Plain Chachalaca*

2. *Red-throated Caracara*

3. *Red-capped Manakin*

4. *Brush Turkey*

5. *White-headed Marsh-Tyrant*

6. *Hooded Oriole*

7. *Cactus Wren*

8. *Broad-billed Hummingbird*

9. *Pyrrhuloxia*

10. *Curve-billed Thrasher*

13. *Arctic Tern*

11. *Steller's Jay*

12. *Broad-tailed Hummingbird*

14. *Tropical Parula*

15. Anna's Hummingbird

17. Blue Dachis

16. Rufous Hummingbird

18. Yellow-bellied Sapsucker

19. Northwestern Crow

20. Red Phalarope

22. *Pine Grosbeak*

21. *Brahminy Kite*

23. *Long-tailed Jaeger*

24. *Black-headed Grosbeak*

25. Green-headed Tanager

26. Bare-faced Ibis

27. Red-breasted Toucan

28, Turquoise-browed Motmot

29. Greater Flamingo

30. Purple-throated Mountain-gem

31. Blue-faced Honeyeater

32. Fork-tailed Flycatcher

33. Savannah Hawk

34. Brown Kiwi

35. New Zealand Pigeon

36. Forest Kingfisher

37. Rainbow Bee-eater

38. Swallow-tailed Gull (im.)

39. Rainbow Bee-eater

40. *Galapagos Hawk*

41. *Crowned Crane*

42. *Superb Starling*

43. *Indigo Bunting*

44. *Lesser Flamingo*

45. Crab Plover

46. Blue-eared Starling

47. Red-billed Hornbill

48. Ground Hornbill

49. Marabou Storks

50. Chaffinch

51. Rose-breasted Grosbeak

52. White-throated Kingfisher

53. Summer Tanager

54. *My nesting Painted Bunting*

55. *Great Crested Grebe*

56. *Great Reed Warbler*

57. Pied Water-Tyrant

58. Fiscal Shrike

59. Giant Petrel

60. Hooded Vulture

61. *Long-tailed Shrike*

62. *Cape Gannet*

63. *Martial Eagle (im.)*

64. *California Condor*

65. *Great Black-Hawk*

66. *Jim with Texas Indigo Snake*

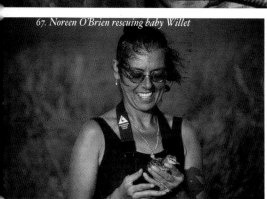

67. *Noreen O'Brien rescuing baby Willet*

68. *Caribou crossing Dalton Highway*

69. *Jim with (foreground left to right) Richard Mayfield, Maureen Myers, Elsie Smith, David Sibley*

I sat there watching this marvelous creature for at least a half-hour, with my head telling me I needed to go find more life birds, and my heart making me sit tight. Once again, I had that conflicted question raised, about the importance of every life bird. In the end, it was the cock who settled things, by flying back into the woods, out of sight.

It had been a wonderful day around Machu Picchu, but it was time to take the train back. It was neat being around tourists who were from every country on earth. I heard French, English in both Brit and Aussie style, German, Japanese and some middle-eastern language unknown to me. All this, of course was with Spanish in the background, as well as some "dialectos" used by several natives. So, after a hot supper and some field guide study, it was off to bed for an early start.

The next morning I was up and off to the road up the Andes to Abra Malaga Pass well before sunup. The switchback road wound back and forth on the western, dry slope of the Andes, getting cooler by the minute. Several stops were made to identify birds flitting along the road, many of which I had been expecting from my night-time study. Eventually, I left the trees behind, and the montane "tundra" had even more new species. One of my favorites was the miner, who hops along turning over rocks, presumably looking for bugs. These terrestrial turn-stones were bland in color, but rich in personality.

Finally, near the top of the pass, it was time to look for condors. Following the cock-of-the-rock yesterday, this was the last of my target birds, those five I just had to see. I've always had pretty sharp eyes, and they worked overtime this morning, scanning both ways for Mr. Megavulture. After two hours, I decided to move to the other side of the pass, but was not at all prepared for what I found.

Apparently, the prevailing winds here are out of the east, and they carry vast amounts of moisture onto the east side of the Andes from Amazonas. This produces cloud forests at the upper latitudes and rain forests at the lower elevations. But on the side from whence I just came, it was dry and without much vegetation. So, I drove up to the top of the pass, and absolutely couldn't believe my eyes. First, puffs of moist clouds streamed into my windshield, floating off well above the "rain shadow" of the west side. But in front of me was lush vegetation, beckoning me to discover its avian secrets.

I stepped out into the chilly mountain air and was almost simultaneously greeted with a flurry of activity. Amazingly, though, these birds were bright red! They were Scarlet-bellied Mountain-Tanagers, a gaudy, exquisite bird that seemed everywhere. For the next few minutes I just wandered down the road, into huge cloud forest trees, and was astounded at the variety of birds. For the rest of the day, I worked slowly down the slope, adding an amazing number of life birds to my list, and treasuring every moment of this lush forest.

This road would require more than one day. I arose very early the next morning, and took no time speeding to the top of Abra Malaga Pass. It was only getting light in the east, through the fog, and I reveled at surely being the only human for many miles. Then, suddenly, I was standing only a few feet from some man, with binoculars and a tape recorder. That was a shock. He was obviously listening to one especially loud bird (that I would not have recognised by voice), so I approached and whispered, "What's that bird?" In an answer that will always be one of my favorite moments in all my birding, he looked at me with big eyes and spoke in a hushed tone, "It's a Supercilliated Hemisphengis."

Holding back a chuckle at such a wonderful name, I held out my hand to introduce myself. He was Tom Schulenberg, and had probably forgotten more about Andean birds than I'll ever know. He was friendly enough, and allowed me to tag along. Another rather loud bird sang out of the shadows. He remarked that it was an Inca Wren, and I immediately popped open my field guide to see what it looked like. With a conciliatory voice, he told me the bird wasn't in my book, that it was new to science. New to science? Wow.

After I left, it troubled me somewhat that I was out bird listing for personal pleasure, and Tom was contributing to the knowledge of science. We had supper together that evening, and once again there was that sinking feeling that I'd rather be doing what he was doing, than just beefing up my life list. He offered that I was accomplishing a lot for science through my teaching, but I just wasn't satisfied. This whole line of thinking stayed with me for days, and actually, for the rest of my life.

My last destination in Peru was the eastern slope of the Andes about 100 miles south of Cuzco. The drive down was a cold one, through icy puddles and bitter winds. This was especially true since this was the heart of the Austral winter. As I approached the part where the road eased down the Andes, I was greeted by the same Scarlet-bellied Mountain-Tanagers as before. What gems they were! They looked like little ornaments on the windswept trees, and the nippy conditions didn't seem to phase them.

The road, which eventually leads to Puerto Maldonado, began innocuously enough, but deep ruts began appearing after the first two or three curves. The road was red clay, and quite slippery. I had to keep my right tires on the high ridge between the deepening ruts, and the left ones along the high outer edge of the road. I must say, it made me feel uncomfortable peering out my window and down. Well, never mind that: I was scared out of my mind! It was certainly a prescription for disaster, but by this time, I had little choice but to continue. There was no turning around.

For several miles, my foot never touched the gas pedal. Gravity eased me down, and most of the time first gear helped slow the process. There were several places by forest clumps to stop and bird. At one such location, I simply couldn't believe my eyes. On a limb out over a small brook, there was — sitting side by side — a male cock of the rock, and a male quetzal. Never have so much beauty and color been compacted in one area.

The road improved toward the bottom, and there were many opportunities for life birds. I camped in the hills that evening, drove the roads for snakes and goatsuckers, and really had the time of my life. The people of the town of Marcapata were very nice, and we swapped snake stories and bird lore several times. It was a tough area to leave, and I also was nervous about the ascent to the top over the road from Hades. As is often the case, things are never as bad as the anticipation of doom, and I found that driving up bad roads aren't as bad as driving down.

A chilly drive brought me to Cuzco, and the equally chilling thought that I had only one more opportunity to see condors. I would be taking a different road back, this one to San Juan on the Pacific coast. I returned to Cuzco, headed west to Abancay, and overnighted in a cheap hotel.

The next morning was a bright blue, crisp day in the Austral winter. I headed out of town with some chicken and fruit, hoping to make San Juan by nightfall. Moreover, I was hoping to finally see my condor. This was the number one desire of mine coming to South America, and this was clearly my last shot. There wasn't a huge variety of birds on the puna zone, but many were fun to see. Later in the morning, I began to wonder where the gas stations were, as I was getting well down below half. Then a quarter full. Then, things began to really get serious. I was nearing the big E and there wasn't a sign of civilization. Boy, where's AAA when you need them?

I didn't know it at the time, but I had about 80 miles to go, and I would have never made it. But as I bounced along the icy road, I came upon another idiot out in the middle of nowhere, and — get this — his VW had a flat tire. Well, I lent him my spare and he put some gas into my car from a jerry can, and together, we limped into Nazca. That wasn't the best part, though.

No less than three times I saw a large bird in the air that could have been a condor. The first time it sailed behind a mountain never to be seen again. The second one was heading dead into the opposite direction, and I could only speculate if it was my greatest avian desire. The third bird looked like a distinct possibility, but when I slammed on brakes, it took several seconds for the dust cloud to settle, and the bird was gone, as I was peering right into the intense sun. This was one of the most frustrating moments of the trip for me. I was being teased by the condor god, and the last mountain top was dead ahead. After that, it was no more condor possibilities.

This last shot proved to be just what the bird doctor ordered, though. Here is part of my entry from July 23:

Then it happened. Fate finally kissed me. With the sun at my back, I saw a huge form, still overhead, and was out of my car in a flash. It was a huge form, riding the waves of air created by the mountains. I focused my binocams on infinity, and found the sharp image in the heavens. It was a monstrous figure, solid black, with a distinct white neck ruff. Then it wheeled, revealing the broad, white stripe on the top of each five-foot wing. Finally, it was an Andean Condor!

I jubilantly jumped, stomped the dirt, kicked shut the car door, and war-whooped all the way to San Juan. I watched the great beast for timeless minutes, studying its moves and reveling in its majesty. It was an organic piece of art Boeing could never duplicate. I absolutely stood awestruck, a happy prisoner of time and space. The wonder of life had once again suspended all else that mattered, and focused my whole being on this magnificent monument to Life on Earth.

Aside from that, it was a pretty ordinary afternoon.

VENEZUELA

Returning to Lima, I cleaned up, returned the recently ventilated VW to its rather dumbfounded owner (and a foxy lady she was), and flew to Caracas, Venezuela. Here I was to make the acquaintance of one Mary Goodwin, whom I had contacted back in May via her ABA address. As I left Peru, there was a bit of a letdown, as I had seen the five biggies I wanted, and frankly, nothing could top the adventure. What could Venezuela possibly have that could compete with anacondas and condors?

Mary was out of town when I arrived in Caracas, so I headed out into the mountains along the north coast. It was just an extension of the Andes, curving way around to the east, but it had many birds new to me. Here I saw my first manakins of South America, and these cute little buggers just delighted my heart. I got into a lek, and the males were just obsessed with performing their best stuff for the lady.

Soon I left for Rancho Grande, in Henry Pitter National Park, via bus. Oh man, what a place! I began at the top, where birds were simply everywhere. This area has more birds than anywhere in the New World, and that wasn't hard to believe. Moreover, there are twice as many bird species in Venezuela than all of North America. Tanagers were thick as thieves, various parrots sat lounging around on nearby limbs, various furnariids crept along the branches and trunks like a huge band of creepers, and Howler Monkeys just about blasted my ears out. With as impressive as the colorful birds were, the wall of sound all around me was astounding. My favorite bird of the day was the Swallow-Tanager, but a forest falcon ranked up pretty high.

I worked this road for two days, walking north to the Caribbean one day and south toward Maracay the other. The third day was a weekend, so I cleverly avoid the onslaught of traffic and worked the old road to the east. Life birds still came early and often, and I wondered how many hundreds I had tallied since I arrived June 6.

I birded this area for two more days, and returned to Caracas to organize a shared taxi to Calabozo. This new location was far from mountainous. This is the llanos, the flooded backwaters from the Orinoco River. My first destination was the Guarico River, home of the indescribable Pale-headed Jacamar. The river being shallow, and with high wooded edges, the simple plan was to wade the river. I hid a few valuables under the bridge, and carefully eased into the alluvial waters.

It really was a lovely stroll downstream, with several kingfishers darting by, raptors in the air, and various songbirds working along the river's bank. Life birds came easy, and most individuals afforded great looks. It was usually around waste deep, although a few spots had water up to my chest. But what a great vantage point to see the workings of a tropical river!

Following the fourth turn in the river, I discovered the delicious jacamar peeping loudly and protesting my arrival. I got great looks, and finally was diverted by a Band-backed Wren that was simply the most handsome wren the world has to offer. Not far down the river, though, I ran into two very exercised fishermen, and they seemed to want to talk to me — big-time!

I was afraid that I was trespassing, though this is rare in tropical countries. As I approached, I distinctly heard the word "peligro," and I was wondering what was so dangerous. They explained to me that there were piranha in the river, and that I would soon be attacked. Bummer. Then, they also said there were Orinoco Crocodiles that would eat me alive, and I knew those little heads I'd been slipping by were nothing more than harmless caimen. The sidekick insisted that there were landlocked stingrays around me, and electric eels as well. Sounded like my kind of place.

I was getting ready to leave the river anyway, so about fifty yards downstream (I didn't want them to think they had scared me out of the river) I began finding a place to exit up the far bank. It was slippery enough, but sure beat trying to drag a monstrous snake with me. Holding onto various plants, I pulled my soaking wet torso up the bank and onto the grassy top. It was then that I had one of the truly hideous experiences of my life.

I had leeches. Oh, my god, I was literally covered with leeches, mostly on my legs, and under my shirt. I mean, those bloodsuckers were all over me, stem to stern. I tend to be pretty cavalier about most things like this, but being covered with wormy vampires was more than I could take. Being hidden between bushes, and it being a very warm day, I began shedding clothes and leeches at quite a clip. When I'd grab a leech with my fingertips and pull it off, they'd just latch onto my fingers, so I created an alternate solution.

I picked up a large, empty metal can and scraped them off me and into the can (counting those nasties as I dumped them in). When I was finished, I kid you not, I had picked off seventy-three leeches! I redressed, closed the lid on the can, and left those slimy bloodsuckers right out in the hot sun. I'll bet it must have sucked to be them!

Reluctantly putting on sopping wet clothes, I at least didn't feel the noontime tropical heat for a while. The birding was still pretty good, though, but my two granola bars I'd been hoarding were even better. There were many flycatchers around to sort out, some finches and sparrows in the field adjacent to the river, and a number of tropical hawks were soaring by this time. They seemed especially active between midmorning and the early afternoon thunder boomers.

Speaking of which, just about the time I got dry, the rains rolled in. I hid under a huge tree, but still got fairly wet. I hunched over to protect my binocams, and other valuables. Within a half-hour, the deluge was over, and it soon became hot again, with an even higher humidity. I

birded this riverine area and its gallery forests for the balance of the day, and headed into Calabozo for supper around sundown. The dinner was quite tasty, but I could have done without the excitement of reaching into my pocket for change and coming out with a leech on my thumb. Make that seventy-four.

The next day I took the bus down to the ranch of Señor Thomas Blohem, a close friend of Mary Goodwin. This was a wonderful experience! His ranch is simply replete with birdlife, with lots of Hoatzin, tiger-herons, gallinules, wintering shorebirds, Bare-faced Ibis [no.26], and oodles of White-faced Whistling-Ducks. Land birds were just as abundant, including quite a few species I had yet to see. Amazingly, with a lot of hard work, I recorded 47 life birds that day wandering his property.

One of these birds, which I have since seen in more likely places, was a Harpy Eagle — not really belonging on the llanos. This was a huge creature, flying past me just ahead of a rainstorm. There was no doubt about the identity, with its gray head with a black crest, and bold chest band. I felt it was necessary to tell the researchers stationed there about it, although I predicted their skepticism. They should have been skeptical, and it was the only bird I saw the entire summer out of place. However, I later learned that other harpies had been seen in August flying southeast over the llanos.

Harpy Eagles have become quite rare in the past fifty years in tropical America, due to deforestation and other human intervention. They are the largest of the world's eagles, and incredibly powerful creatures. Their larger-than-life feet and talons are used to snatch monkeys out of

◀ *White-faced Whistling Ducks*

treetops, where the harpies fly them to safe eating grounds and have them for lunch (this, after crushing their skulls with their talons). This and the extremely endangered Great Philippine Eagle are really two of a kind, and such magnificent birds should be preserved at all costs.

There were other neat animals on Señor Thomas' property. He raises Orinoco Crocodiles, an endangered species in northern South America. Looking at least as prehistoric were massive Green Iguanas, except that the males were more red than green. They reminded me of the iguanas of the Galapagos, which, of course, evolved from Greens which floated out to the islands on trees millennia ago. I also ran upon a very large Tropical Rattlesnake, a monstrous "diamondback" with stripes on the neck, just behind the head. Their bite is much worse than our diamondbacks of North America, but, of course, I couldn't resist the temptation to catch it. The answer to your question is, "because it was there."

Also at Señor Thomas's ranch, I made the acquaintance of two graduate researchers, David and Peter. They were mostly working on Hoatzins, and apparently had been for quite some time. They had absolutely come to hate that bird, and the reason was, well, elementary (Hoatson) — they were sick and tired of these crazy beasts, which seemed to be half bird and half reptile. They loathed them, they had nothing but insults for them, but continued their work toward a further advanced degree. They did do a fair amount of research on weekends on sexual selection of the genus Homo, as the reddish color in their eyes always indicated the next morning (when I was instructed to not raise my voice). Seriously though, I so wanted to tell them how lucky they were that their research would add to the body of knowledge of science, far more than my list, which would sit on a shelf and collect dust.

Upon leaving I hitched a ride south to San Fernando, where I ate like a tyrannosaur, and took a hot shower. From, there, I got another ride west to an area called "El Frio," which was suppose to be great for llanos birds. Apparently, the land is slightly higher than the flatlands everywhere else, and it's about one degree cooler, with a fair breeze. What really cracks me up is that the locals who pass this way put on a jacket going through El Frio, with such frigid temperatures. I have noticed this phenomenon in other places in the tropics around the world, where a few degrees means a whole lot more to those living in tropical climates than it ever will to those of us from temperate latitudes.

El Frio was a lovely place to observe waterbirds, with Jabiru, Capped Heron (now, there's a beautiful bird), five species of ibis, lovely Whistling Herons, Maguari Storks, loads of whistling ducks and my first Comb Duck. Raptors were also abundant in this area, with my favorite being the common but beautiful Savannah Hawk [no.33]. There were also White-headed Marsh-Tyrants [no.5], Black-collared Hawks in the ditches (I believe they prefer water), Aplomado Falcons racing across the sky, Great Black-Hawks (who also seem to like water), Lesser Yellow-headed Vultures (with several pseudonyms) and one handsome King Vulture. Lastly, speaking of vultures, they were frequently found with caracaras ripping animal remains off the hot roads, in gruesome but biological efficiency.

It was tough leaving the llanos, but I knew my time in Venezuela was getting short, and I wanted to try hooking up with Mary one more time. I therefore arranged a hired taxi back to Caracas, and began calling the Goodwin residence.

Finally meeting Mary face to face was a treat. She was not young, but had the energy of five men. Apparently, she has been a human dynamo for Venezuelan conservation, not making a whole lot of friends with the bureaucracy. Her knowledge of the country's birds was only exceeded by her obvious love for and commitment to them, and she earned my respect and admiration immediately. She and her baseball-loving husband took me in for the night, but unfortunately, she was still recovering from an illness, and couldn't go birding with me. But boy, did she have an alternate plan!

She asked why I didn't head down to La Gran Sabana, and absolutely loaded my wagon with superlatives about how great it was. The area has lowland rain forest like the

Guayanan Trail, great riverine forests like the Rio Grande, and more good birding all the way down to El Dorado. Then, the road climbs through the heavily-forested side of the first Tepui, the oldest mountains on Earth. These huge, tabletop structures are Precambrian, sandstone formed before there was life on Earth.

The road up to the top, called the Escalera, passes through each life zone from lowland Amazonas to cloud forest, and offers chances for many of the great birds of northern South America. Often known as the Lost World, it is likely the final resting place of famous pilot Johnny Angel, the namesake of Angel Falls (in the heart of the Lost World).

Needless to say, I was so excited I could hardly sleep. I arrived at the airport early the next morning, flew to Ciudad Guiana, and rented a truck. Off I went to the Rio Grande, several hours away (after a stop for provisions for the next few days). I didn't arrive at the Rio Grande until well after dark, but the road was strewn with all kinds of neat snakes. There was the coral snake that has a red nose, Fer-de-Lance, Tropical Rattlesnakes, several rat snake types and one huge Bushmaster. So cool!

Dawn came early on the dirt road that passes through the Rio, and my ears were inundated with the tropical wall of sound. Of particular import were the amazingly loud Gray-winged Trumpeters, who were strutting right out into the road, matching a rock band decibel for decibel. Still, I couldn't wait to get into the forest and find a flock. Watching for fanged nasties, I slipped through the foliage and within three minutes stood face to face with a White-plumed Antbird. Others of this wonderful group were to

◀ *Maguari Stork*

follow, with many such as antpitta beginning with the name of the insects they follow. It was sure hard to beat the lovely little Ringed Antpipit, though.

Once in a good flock of antbirds, I watched as the various species follow Army Ants through the forest, grabbing insects scared up by the predatory ants. They worked well together, like the diving birds and hovering gulls I once saw off Cape Flattery, chasing fish. Even a hard-core lister such as myself had to suspend ticking off lifers for a few minutes and just watch the forest drama unfold.

I also enjoyed canopy birding at Rio Grande, where I eventually laid on my back, propped against a clump of dirt, picking out tanagers and their kin high in the lowland rain forest canopy. Tanagers were like the warblers of North America, with their diversity only exceeded by their colors. Still, one of my favorites was the Magpie

Tanager, a black and white creature fairly common in field edges near the Rio Grande. This also afforded looks at tinamou, trogons, toucans, and about any other tropical bird that begins with "t."

Soon it was time to head south, to the lovely Guayanan Trail, for rain forest birding in another ecotone. This was the secret path on which refugees used to go back and forth between Guayana and Venezuela when times were worse. One remnant from those days is the English many people speak in this small area, which, I must admit, was nice to hear. It was on this trail that a male Guyanan Cock-of-the-Rock sat in full view for this excited spectator. Not far down the trail was a Black Nunbird, also a remarkable creature. I really left this area too early, but I was in quite a hurry to get to the Escalera.

Upon arriving at El Dorado, I secured a cheap room and rode out a typical Saturday night in the tropics. It was loud, and it went on (seemingly) all night long. A little sleepy the next morning, I dragged myself out of bed, and took off up the mountainside for one of the truly great days of my life. Each stop seemed to have new birds, with lowland species eventually disappearing and those of higher elevations being found at various points up the road. I worked this road for three days, and never seemed to stop seeing life birds. My favorite bird for Venezuela was the Capuchinbird, which was kind enough to swoop down in front of me, and sit out in plain sight for thirty seconds. I also really enjoyed arriving at the top of the Escalera and hearing the unmistakable gong of the bellbird, being a reminder of the species Dr. Skutch showed me so many years before.

◀ *Tepui mountains*

The top of the Tepui mountain was suddenly flat and grassy, as far as the eye could see. The third day I took the road south, and the scenery became more and more gorgeous with each passing mile. Indescribably beautiful rivers cut across the road from east to west in a few places, with some absolutely magnificent waterfalls offering stunning vistas to those few folks who braved the frontier. Being a new road, word was not "out" about this enchanted part of Venezuela, but on subsequent trips, I noticed more and more traffic.

After several hours of driving, and at least that many birding in wooded canyons, I reached the town of Santa Elena, right on the Brazilian border. Getting out of my truck, I was shocked at how cold it had gotten just after sundown, although two large rattlesnakes had just slithered off the road. This was to be the far end of my journey, and the next day's birding found yet more species for my list.

Birds seen on the Escalera during the return trip that most impressed me were flocks of Paradise Tanagers, macaws, the wonderful Sharpbill, many new species of hummingbirds, White Hawks, several new woodcreepers, a dazzling array of furnariids, more antbirds, and confusing flycatchers.

There were certainly colorful birds as well, though, like the Pompadour Cotinga, Red-banded Fruiteater, Pink-throated Becard, Red-legged Honeycreeper, Blue Dacnis, Opal-rumped Tanager, Blue-naped Chlorophonia, White-winged and Blue-backed tanagers, and many others. It was with a heavy heart that I head north, dreaming of the day I once again work the Escalera. Little did I know that my life-long quest for 5000 birds would end on this hallowed mountain.

After quite a drive, I arrived in Caripe, home of the bizarre Oilbird. These relatives of our goatsuckers live in caves, and echolocate like bats through their mazes. They emerge at night and snatch fruit off limbs, taking the food back to their cave youngsters. They received their names because earlier humans would ring out the young (of course killing them) and take their oil (fat) to light lamps. The main oil bird cave is a bit of a tourist spot, but it seems well run. Evenings are chilly, but if one is patient, oilbirds will appear in droves near dark, foraging in the local hillsides.

The countryside is strewn with coffee plantations, which are pretty good places for birds. Walking the roads the next two days yielded many new birds, but sadly, the trip was winding down. Soon, it was time to drive the coastal road back to Caracas, bid farewell to my new friend Mary, and begin thinking about mundane things like classrooms and mortgage payments.

The trip back was about what I expected: hassles at the airport, melodramatic people so glad I was home safe, and the sinking feeling that I'd rather be out in the jungle. On the positive side, my life list was now more than two thousand, and I was well on my way to my goal. The months of work ahead were best summarized at the end of my 234-page journal I kept, where I closed with:

> And what of the trip? The Bible says that to find your life, you must lose it. In a different vein, though, I found my life in the Lost World of the Gran Sabana,

and I now return to lose myself in the teaching about life in my other world. I may feel a little down now, but I will climb the Escalera again.

And indeed, I have.

CHAPTER FIVE

AUSTRALIA: LAND OF THE UNIQUE

Following my return from South America, I couldn't wait to get back to the New World Tropics and fill in some holes in my life list. Trips to Guatemala and several locations in South America were crammed into summers and Christmas holidays, so my life list rose in bits and pieces during this time. My list stood at 2317 when I made my first trip to the Eastern Hemisphere, to the great land down under.

At this point in my professional life, I really needed the diversion of birding trips. I taught an overload, often with well over thirty students per class, and served my high school on several committees, such as chairing the school improvement team. This was no easy task, with an administration which was frankly reluctant to admit there were any deficiencies at my Alma Mater. This put me in the line of fire between the teachers and the principals, and caused me to begin feeling great stress for the first time in my (now rather) young life. Still, my devotion to the students, and the school I loved, kept me coming back for more.

One hiatus that became a regular custom was the "Galveston Island Trip" I began running nearly every spring. This area had been recommended to me by my dad, with wild tales of thousands of songbird migrants dropping all over the beaches and dunes, and it was a place I had to go. My first trip out was solo, and I discovered the loveliest little patch of forest up on a man-made hill on the desolate west end of the barrier island.

In subsequent years, I took bird-watching students with me, and we often camped inside the trees in this almost surreal location. One trip out, we had some equipment stolen, and we dubbed the place "Heartbreak Hammock." Ironically, I would one day take my broken heart back to this place and find permanent happiness in the woodsy patch of paradise.

June 3, 1987 couldn't come soon enough. A local college professor named Liz boarded the big bird with me, and we roared off to the Eastern Hemisphere. Our first stop was Hawaii, which was a singularly wonderful experience. One day we drove around the big island, stopping at forest patches and admiring Mother Nature's volcanic work. We even visited my cousin David and his wonderful wife, Trish. Working in Hawaii was a tough job that somebody had to do.

We spent several days in paradise, visiting the high mountains, seeing the colorful finches Darwin missed, and getting very wet in the area of greatest rainfall in the world. We saw tropicbirds floating effortlessly on mountain updrafts, touched the majestic Silversword, and stood within a few feet of a lovely White Tern. My stress level had returned to zero, and my good friend Liz was such an easy person with whom to travel.

We left at midnight the fourth day for the land of Dundees and pouches. There was a bright moon peeping out through the clouds that night, offering a surreal image that would have made Halloween proud. Later, not long before first light, I spotted the Southern Cross, a sure sign this wasn't Kansas. It also didn't take Oz's Wizard to know that this was going to be one long flight. I am still saddened by the fact that an older man not far in front of us died that night, and I also remember the crew trying to break things to the passengers carefully. What a night!

The deal we had was a round trip flight to Australia, several domestic flights around the Kangaroo Country, and a stop in New Zealand, all for $1100. We were landing in Melbourne and heading out from there, and my excitement level hadn't come out of the heavens yet. I immediately fell in love with Australia — the people, the countryside and especially the birds.

In a lot of other destinations, the first birds I see are House Sparrows, pigeons, starlings and Cattle Egrets. Here, my first Australian sighting was a flock of pink birds — parrots, to be exact — called Galahs. Oh, my! In fact, I soon realized that the Psittaciformes — those of the parrot order — were widespread and abundant. I saw Galahs everywhere, several species of gaudy rosellas, long, slender parrots, Cockatiel, huge cockatoos (some white and some black) and even the Budgerigar of my childhood bird cages.

The mountains along the eastern edge of Australia were

lovely, and being there in the Austral winter allowed for pleasant temperatures. It also meant that the terrible family of Elapidae snakes, easily the most deadly in the world, might be snoozing underground while we tramped through the woods. Those woods, containing about 500 species of gum trees (Eucalyptus), had many more birds than just kookaburras that "sits" on them. Splendid kingfishers, beautiful robins (flycatchers), bizarre wattlebirds, gleaming sunbirds and loads of honeyeaters all sits on the old gum trees.

On my "most wanted" list were the two lyrebird species, renowned imitators of everything. We found one male holding court in Royal National Park near the parking lot, and he gave more imitations than an army of mockingbirds. Nothing could have prepared me for what was next on tap, when Liz went to use the lady's room — that bird actually recreated the sound of the toilet flushing!

Just as the mammals have evolved uniquely on Earth in this disjunct land, there are also quite an array of odd birds for the unfamiliar outlander. One favorite group was the Malleefowl and Brush Turkey [no.4], two confirmed mound builders. They rake up huge piles of debris, lay their eggs in the middle, and allow the heat of decomposition to incubate their eggs. They even return at intervals to check on the temperature, and adjust the egg position and cover to keep them at the correct heat index.

Being a raptor lover, it was nice seeing the Whistling Kites everywhere, especially around areas where fields were being burned. They apparently grab fleeing varmints, and perhaps the charred remains of creatures who didn't

Wedge-tailed Eagle ▶

escape the flames. Alas, a creature who loved Crispy Critters as much as I did as a child.

These fires, used to recycle nutrients back into the soil, brought up a somewhat embarrassing moment for me. I was with several Aborigines, when one of them asked what was new in the world of science in America. Feeling like a god who was bringing The Word down from heaven to some primitive savages, I shared about our country's new understanding of control burning (prescribed fires), and all the wonderful things we'd learned that fire does to the natural ecosystem. Noticing that they were surprisingly quiet, one of the younger ones said in a disappointed voice, "Yeah, we've been doing that for about forty thousand years," So much for this god.

I especially love eagles, and the Wedge-tailed Eagles of Australia were delightful. Closely related to our Golden Eagles, they are fearless hunters and great fliers.

Somewhat less exciting were the sea eagles, but one that snatched up a barramunda from a billabong did provide a compelling moment for this falconiphile.

Another interlude of wonder brought me face to face with avian legends of old. I was watching a honeyeater work its way slowly through the low limbs, and suddenly stop to feed a fat little bird that obviously wasn't his progeny. Duuh! I was watching one of the famous old world brood parasites (a bronze-cuckoo) being raised by a willing but ignorant surrogate parent. This bit of biology, that I could take back to "my kids" on tape in biology, made me feel like David Attenborough.

Other lovelies of the eastern woods included the colorful little pittas, the delightful and amazingly colorful fairy wrens, the Forest Kingfishers [no.36], Blue-faced honeyeaters [no.31], Shining Starlings, and the orioles, which have traded their yellows of the New World for delicious greens and reds.

The Blue Mountains of Eastern Australia gave us great looks at bowerbirds, who steal any shiny object they can find and decorate their breeding chambers for prospective mates. These odd-looking bowers resemble perhaps a pawn shop's trash pile, but seem to attract the bowergal's attention just fine.

Somewhat related were the astoundingly beautiful riflebirds, famous for their resounding calls. These relatives of nearby New Guinea's birds-of-paradise have a whistling sound that is reminiscent of a bullet ricocheting, and seems to reverberate through the canopy like a vocalized guided missile.

Another real "looker" that I admired was the drongo, an

iridescent-black creature with a long tail and red eyes of steel. My first encounter found one perched motionless among the gum tree limbs until one of many wren species came flitting by. Suddenly, the drongo swooped off its hiding place and smashed into the hapless nymph like a Bat Falcon. This was no ordinary black bird.

The freshwater marsh birds were exciting as well. Wading birds such as the Black-necked Stork, Sarus Crane, spoonbills and the monstrous Great-billed Heron all reminded me of New World marshes that I loved so much. But the most incredible wading bird wasn't in a marsh at all.

Liz and I arose early one morning in the Iron Range and crammed our belongings in the jeep while it was still dark. She apparently placed a bunch of aging bananas in a box behind her, where I later stuck my camera for easy access. Off we went, over a hot and dusty road, only to come to a deep stream we had to cross.

No sooner than I had eased the jeep out into the flowing waters did I look up and see the very rare Black Bittern standing not eight feet away on a branch. He was obviously considering flight, but being a bittern, was pondering camouflage as well. I gulped and quietly mentioned the bird to Liz, as I slid my hand back to pull out my trusty camera. As the macro lens passed my face, my eyes and nose both realized instantly that there was a problem. There was banana goo all over the lens!

Oh, man! With Liz fumbling for every Kleenex she could unearth (God bless women), I furiously wiped the glass clean, while watching the nervous bird's anxieties grow. As soon as I felt it appropriate, I slowly turned toward the bird with camera up, and squeezed off a shot right as the bird took off like an Apollo rocket. I didn't know until returning home that the picture froze him perfectly on the limb, albeit with somewhat of a dingy aspect to it!

While in the Atherton Tablelands, I couldn't pass up the opportunity to search for the world's most poisonous creature — the Small-scaled Snake (or Green Taipan). It lives near cracks in the age-old sandstone and strikes mice and other small animals with its unbelievably potent venom, keeping them from escaping into a crack. Death would be instantaneous, and was reportedly nearly so for humans as well (the Aborigine refer to this small serpent as "that little bastard"). Naturally, you can see why I'd want to catch one.

The only person to have survived this beast's wrath was a herpetologist who led a team to these parts years earlier, as the snake was mostly known through Abo myth, and many doubted its actual existence. As the story goes, they

finally found one, and as the leader was showing it off, the snake managed to graze one finger with a fang. The poor fellow collapsed unconscious and was flown by helicopter to Melbourne. He allegedly died twice aboard the chopper, was stabilized, lived in a coma for six months, and finally recovered use of most of his body. That's some bite! I was fortunate enough to find one within a couple of days (while adding life birds galore), and plopped it down in a shady opening for a picture. They look a bit like the nasty old Green Water Snakes I used to catch in Lake Jackson, just north of Tallahassee. This snake may be more poisonous, but I doubt anything could hurt as badly as those aquatic leviathans (anything except anacondas).

The Elapidae family was all over Australia, with King Browns, other taipans, Death Adders and the famous Tiger Snakes. There were also a few colubrids, the non-poisonous family comprising about 85% of all snake species worldwide, but my favorite snakes were the Water Pythons. These were gentle giants, fairly common, and quite inoffensive. We saw nine in about an hour of road cruising, and just had a ball making friends with these scaley puppy dogs.

Meanwhile, back at the Australian ranch, it was time to head west. Our first stop was a wonderful marshy area called Fogg Dam. We walked down the earthen dike and there were hundreds of cockatoos (actually, Long-billed Corellas) in the road and trees, with the marsh being loaded with a thousand Pied Geese, several species of new ducks, and two wonderful little Green Pygmy-Geese. The weird thing about Fogg Dam was the inescapable feeling

◀ *Black Bittern*

of déja vu. Obviously, I had never been here before, but how was it so familiar?

In an hour or so, I walked up to a small store on the corner for a soda, and shared my mystery with the store keeper. He smiled and said that the opening scene of Crocodile Dundee was shot there, when Mick made the Water Buffalo lie down, and all that. Realizing that I wasn't crazy after all, I went back to birding, and soon found myself photographing a marvelous Little Eagle.

Nearby Kackadoo National Park was vast and beautiful, though perhaps not as birdy as some other places. The boat ride on the South Alligator River is a must, though, and some of the Estuarine Crocodiles are unimaginably huge. After dark, they came quite close to the boat landings, and their red eyes could be seen by flashlight easily. I decided to give them a break and let them be.

I went out the second night in the park after dark to look for snakes and other nocturnal delights, and had the scare of a lifetime. I was slowly working my way down a billabong shoreline, checking out these frogs that could easily have passed for the leopard frogs of my childhood.

My mind was so totally engrossed in what was in the beam, I failed to look where I was going. The skinny is that I walked right up to a "salty" (crocodile) so close that he bolted into the water. He may well have thought I was hunting him. For the first and only time in my life, I honestly could not breathe. I had to find a bare spot (carefully) and sit down, with my heart pumping about 160 times a minute. I did keep an eye on the billabong, and when the croc reappeared not too far away, I decided to call it a night. On the bright side, I added two nightjars and an owl to my life list, and still had my life as well.

Through teaching zoology, I have learned a fair amount about the animal kingdom in general, and developed an appreciation for social insects, for instance. These tens of thousands of creatures all living as one have actually been compared to one large animal — say a mammal like an ungulate — all having about the same niche and impact on the environment as that one deer or gazelle. Those termites in Australia build the most amazing homes — like giant cones — and are hard as a rock. How any animal can get beyond their defenses to prey on them is beyond me.

Darwin was a nice break in the "roughing it" of sleeping in a hatchback. The area known as Nightcliff was loaded with shorebirds, and I have never seen such a difference between low and high tides. There were also lots of neat birds around, with my favorites being the Rainbow bee-eaters [nos. 37 & 39]. Darwin had been virtually destroyed by a Christmas Day Hurricane decades ago, but rose from the rubble to become a beautiful city named for the man who understood change as well as anyone. Little did I know that in the mid-90's, my life would undergo such

◀ *Long-billed Corellas*

destruction, only to be rebuilt beyond all previous dreams and expectations.

Returning to Cairns, I birded the Esplanade for shorebirds, which was extremely productive, and gave me many of my first Old World shorebirds. To my absolute utter amazement, there was a familiar face down the shoreline (no, I hadn't seen her on Crocodile Dundee) birding. She was a math teacher from Tallahassee, and would eventually become my wife.

The next day, Liz and I went out to the Great Barrier Reef, and had a wonderful day. There were neat birds, such as a Black Noddy I photographed at about six feet, and lovely little white-eyes in about every tree. The scenery was also exquisite, with the clear blue water and fluffy clouds overhead. My favorite animal of the day though, was a salty behind bars that was 23 feet 6 inches long. That crocodile's head was over five feet long, and when he looked at me, I think he saw lunch.

Another reminder of my Tallahassee home came as I noticed one of the deck hands reading Time of the Turtle, by my good friend Jack Rudloe. They were quite impressed that I knew him and was on the board of directors of Panacea Institute of Marine Science, and they wanted to know more about such an interesting author. I wound up telling them the rather curious story that whenever I went into the field with the Rudloes (Jack and his marine biologist wife, Anne), we always seemed to find a poisonous snake (often in places they'd never seen one), like I attracted the venomous beasts. This led to my asking if we'd likely see a sea snake out on the reef, to which they replied, "No chance."

Having just become acquainted with marine invertebrates, as I recently added marine biology to my teaching load, I couldn't wait to get in the water and see these wonderful creatures first-hand. There were huge sponges acting like invertebrate apartment houses for other creatures, the wildest assortment of colorful anemones, plume worms with incredible detail, bivalves clinging to whatever substrate they could grab, sea cucumbers moving at the speed of drying concrete, quite an array of bizarre crabs, and much more disparity and diversity.

The keystone species in this amazing web was the coral, a relative of the jellyfish and anemones, whose homes stretch contiguously for 1100 miles down the east coast of Australia. Sitting among them was the dreaded Crown-of-thorns Starfish, which is currently eating away at the coral, and threatening the reef itself. Scientists are trying to determine if human activity has had anything to do with this rather drastic situation, but have so far found no connection (I'd put my money on there being one found eventually).

One of the most marvelous moments in my entire life came as I snorkeled up to the edge of the continental shelf, in about four feet of water. You cannot imagine the grandeur of peering over this underwater "cliff" and looking straight down forever. Even in perfectly clear water, there was simply no bottom to be seen. Along the edges of the vertical shelf there were all kinds of animals like lobsters sitting in their little individual niche, poking out only slightly in the spacious abyss. The feeling of insignificance I had at that moment was akin to standing in Canyon del Tigre in Costa Rica, watching a huge, male

Jaguar stalk across the road, or peering into the heavens on a dry Peruvian mountain, watching the massive Andean Condor sailing high above my puny self.

As I floated for several minutes at the door of the deep, I pondered how the search for life birds was taking me into a miraculous laboratory of life around this vast planet. Could there be something else out there as big or greater than the shining, neon "5000?" Surely not. But there was a voice stirring within me, asking silent, unanswered questions about my life's real goals.

At that moment, one more of life's shocks brought me face to face with reality, though only for a fleeting moment. Gently cruising past me, about forty feet out over the precipice, was absolutely the biggest shark I have ever imagined. It's funny how I froze and went into a trance-like state, and yet I remember certain details like they were only a moment ago. The lifeless-looking black pupils, the wicked teeth, and the slow, horizontal waving of the massive caudal fin will remain in my mind as long as I have breath. I was too mesmerized to be scared; I just stared into the oceanic abyss, with the one great player, and could have been on Jupiter for all I knew. I don't know how long he was, but he sure seemed to be going past a long time.

Returning to the boat, my dumb side raised its ugly head again. I had been careful not to touch the coral and other encrusting organisms, especially the fire coral. However, there was one long, high ridge that lay across my path, and I decided I could float over the top if I gulped a large breath of air. I did just that, but as I reached the halfway point passing over, it felt like someone pulled the cork in the sink of the South Atlantic Ocean. I flopped unceremoniously on the coral with my (too) soft belly, and rolled off as gracefully as a whale unbeaching itself.

Needless to say, I got quite the welcoming committee of stares as I returned to the boat – several minutes late. My tardiness was not such an issue as the red marks all across my torso, which I thought was their primary concern. But then the one deck hand who had been reading Jack's book came up and told me that they had just seen the first sea snake in years out there, and it swam right past the boat. That was too ironic.

Returning to Cairns, it was time to go west, young man. We first flew to Alice Springs to see birds of the Outback, and of course, visit mysterious Ayer's Rock. Birding was pleasant, albeit with less the diversity of the perimeter mountains of eastern Australia. I must say, though, that Ayer's Rock was quite a disappointment, as it did not live up to claims. When the sun went down, and I mean as soon as the sun went down, that rock went blacker than night. Glow, my foot!

Our flight out to extreme western Australia brought an entirely different set of birds, even from the Nullarbor Plain. It also afforded us an opportunity to take yet another boat trip, and the oceanic birds just lined up to pose. We went past famous Wive's Island, the tiny rock near Albany where sailors used to leave their wives, to keep them from the evil clutches of local townspeople. When said sailors returned from the sea, they'd pick up their wives, who hadn't dared swim back to shore because of the local Great White Sharks.

My favorite birds down under, and certainly the most

challenging to find, were the Western Bristlebird and the Noisy Scrub-bird. Both are rare and local, occurring only in a small patch of coastal scrub near Two People Bay just east of Albany. The latter is a ventriloquist, seemingly throwing its voice in all directions, while maintaining a low profile. Thought extinct for decades, this small population seemed doomed by a planned housing development, which was bought and paid for. The amazing thing was that once the birds were found, there was no thought whatsoever of building it. Everyone — developers included — agreed this land should be a refuge. With time, both the scrub-bird and the bristlebird made their way to my life list, but not without a lot of searching.

Another one of my favorite birds was Willie Wagtail, a common resident of parks and yards. Their song, often characterized as "sweet pretty creature," warms the hearts of the Aussies, and they even sing on moonlit nights, not unlike the mockingbirds of my neighborhood. However,

decades ago, they became quite rare due to DDT, and the Australian people became very upset at the sharp decline of their little friendly Willie. Again, with no question, courts, lawyers or fanfare, DDT was banned and Willie Wagtail rose to prominence in the yards and hearts of the Australians. Far be it from me to make a controversial comment or comparison, so I'll just let those two examples of environmental concern lie there for all to ponder.

The wonderfully specialized marsupials of the island continent were also fascinating to study. Kangaroos and wallabies were enormously common, and I never got tired of seeing them bound along through the countryside. Echidnas (spiny anteaters) were tough to find, but finally showed themselves not far from Perth. I also got a chance to see the oldest living life forms on earth, the masses of Blue-green Algae, looking superficially like flamingo nests, out in the shallow waters up from where the famed sail boat races are held.

Our side trip to Tasmania was chilly, but quite enjoyable. Russell Falls was indescribably beautiful, with some of the largest and oldest trees in the world. Climbing the mountain road, temperatures dropped sharply, and snow began drifting down from the pearl-white sky. There was a lake at the top that supposedly contained Duck-billed Platypus, one creature I very much wanted to see. The cold walk around the lake was treacherous, with large, slippery boulders covered with lichen and snow. Finally, though, I saw a platypus slipping through the clear water, and squeezed off a shot with my trusty camera. In my moment of triumph, I gazed skyward and discovered a magnificent Wedge-tailed Eagle gliding overhead. To the southwest, an Antarctic cold front swept over my position, with clear skies and strong southwesterly winds behind the trailing edge. Seeing a cold front coming out of the south was about as unlikely as a mammal that lays eggs, and reminded me of how diverse and interesting life on earth actually was.

It was hard to leave the land down under, but I was comforted in the knowledge that I had turned it upside down for every life bird I could have reasonably hoped for. In addition, I must admit a certain fondness for the marsupials of this unique island of zoological history. Darwin may have thought them degenerate, but I found creatures such as Koalas totally adorable.

A short side trip to New Guinea was both fun and full of life birds. On the way from Papua, New Guinea (Port Moresby) to Wau, I actually got to sit in the cockpit and turn the airplane! That was a thrill, but awfully scary. Soon, Liz and I were in the jungle, and I was racking up life birds left and right. What amazed me about New Guinea was how difficult it was to gain a decent look at many of the vocal birds.

I also found it interesting that it is largely a combination of Australian animals that had crossed during the ice ages when ocean levels were low, and plants whose seeds drifted southward over the ocean from Asia. While there, I was mindful of Alfred Russell Wallace, arguably one of the top five biologists of all time. Wallace, a contemporary of Darwin, developed his own idea of natural selection, and sent his findings to Sir Charles. In one of the great class acts of all time, Darwin read Wallace's findings in front of the Royal Society of London alongside his own.

One thing I really wanted to see was a bird-of-paradise courting on a lek. Near Port Moresby, the Raggiana Bird-of-Paradise could be found with some looking, and I made arrangements with a local kid to take me up a mountainside way before dawn one morning to see them on a lek. Getting up at dark-thirty, we trudged up a slick montane path toward our goal, hearing the bird's screams the last few hundred yards. Finally, we reached a clearing, and I got great looks and decent video of this spectacular event. No wonder it's their National Bird.

The people of this area seemed awfully nice, though some were perhaps a little under-motivated. I also noticed their mouths had a distinctive red hue, like they'd been eating redhots, or some such. Well, come to find out they chew betelnut, and it has quite the psychogenic properties. Some of these folks were easy going because they were blasted half out of their minds!

Our last destination for the summer was New Zealand, a land I very much wanted to visit. It reminded me some of Australia, but the forests have been all but replaced with rolling, green pastures. A walk through patches of remaining woods is like returning to Earth in the Paleozoic, with lush, green, soft vegetational undergrowth, and towering, ancient trees. Somehow, the pastures seemed a little less beautiful after walking through what used to be there.

Birds in New Zealand were incredibly tame, with my favorite being the tomtits. There was an unusually high number of introduced birds, like Chaffinches [no.50], but I frankly didn't mind seeing an accentor (it was the last family of North American birds I hadn't seen). The

British settlers seem to enjoy bringing a few birds of their homeland to Anglicize their new domain. I just wonder how we Americans got stuck with House Sparrows, starlings and pigeons.

Our first day we went from Auckland to Miranda, mostly for shorebirds, and what land birds we could happen upon. I enjoyed the honeyeaters and Tui, but the Wrybills stole the day. This creature has a bill that actually curves sideways, built for special mollusks in the mud. There were hundreds of them on one mud flat on the Firth of Thames, and I decided to wade out with my camera, Celestron lens and tripod to take a picture. The eventual slide was even worse than the idea, as I nearly sunk to my waste in muck. Liz was kind enough to take a picture of this defenseless victim of enthusiasm.

Visiting islands brought many native birds, as well as looks at the Tuatara, a primitive "lizard" in its own order of the class Reptilia. They have a third (pineal) eye, and spend much of the day hiding in holes dug in the sides of cliff and outcrops. Holding one was quite a rush, especially in an island country devoid of all snakes. I cannot think of another monotypic order, meaning a taxonomic group that high with only one representative. Next closest is the bizarre Hoatzin, a monotypic family.

We worked our way to the South Island, and it got colder as we went. Finally, we took a boat off the south shore, which surely must rank as one of the coldest days of my life. While others huddled inside the relative warmth of the cabin, I stood out on deck watching Wandering Albatross glide across the sea with ease. It was the Black-browed Albatross an hour or so later that apparently was life bird number 3000, with many more on the trip to come. There were several species of this great family, along with many other pelagic birds to boot. Sometimes birders can get so excited that conditions just don't matter.

There were many birds in New Zealand that I really enjoyed — Paradise Shelduck, New Zealand Pigeon [no.35], and the amazing Kea. But a rainy walk through one particular primeval forest brought me the bird of the trip, for my money. There was no moon, it was quite chilly, and my soggy eyes followed the flashlight beam across the ground for hours. Finally, there it was! It was sneaking through the underbrush, intermittently poking its long bill into the ground for earthworms. I was actually watching a foraging kiwi [no.34]right in front of me. I stood soaked and miserable, but now with the belief that I had accomplished another great trip, and was ready to face the rigors of another year standing and delivering.

CHAPTER SIX

AFRICA: THE DARK CONTINENT

Upon returning from Australia, my life took on some major changes, one in particular. One of my students, Carson Smith, suggested I "take out" her former math teacher from middle school, because we were "just alike." It also occurred to me that she was the daughter of one of my psychology professors from FSU, and he seemed like a

pretty decent guy. So, we went out over the next several months, and decided to get married. Carol was an outstanding math teacher, loved birds very much, and was a beautiful Italian woman.

She had no interest in children of our own, since we both had way too many at school. Therefore, we turned our attention to travel, especially birding. Soon, we were on our way to South America, where we toured the lower half of the continent. The region of Argentina south of Buenos Aires was a wide-open, stark area, replete with wonderful waterfowl and bizarre mammals. My personal favorite memory was sitting on the vast south Atlantic beach with Carol, just having found a penguin, with Giant Petrels [no.59] sailing over the surf, and having her say, "Jim, what's this white gull over here?" Before I even looked, I knew she had found the Snowy Sheathbill I so wanted to see. I will have to say, the sunset that evening was the greatest I have ever seen.

▼ *Snowy Sheathbill*

Our trip up into the Andes was quite a drive. It was cold and windy, but there were many neat birds such as Upland Geese. Photographing an Andean Condor taking food from a Black-chested Buzzard-Eagle was nice. Seeing the Pied Water-Tyrants [no.57] and hearing the Magellanic Woodpecker banging on the monster trees in the Nothofagus forest topped my list of excitement around Bariloche.

Paraguay was an awfully birdy place, with the road into the Chaco providing one neat lifer after another. I especially loved the Pied Water-Tyrant [no.57] and the Great Black Hawks [no.65], although my picture of a Crowned Eagle has brought me satisfaction over the years. What I didn't enjoy was getting so sick I actually had to stay in bed a whole day, and lost that time birding. My temperature rose beyond 102 degrees, and I just wanted to die and get it over with. Finally, after getting unbelievably nause-

Bariloche

ated, my fever broke and I dragged myself out of bed. I was so weak I could hardly walk, which was OK since I was driving. I know that comforted Carol.

Iguassu Falls in Brazil was a real thrill from a tourist standpoint, and there were quite a few new birds in the surrounding forests. We saw this area not long after the movie "Mission," so there was also a historical side. Most amazing to me about the falls itself were the Great Dusky Swifts that literally fly through the waters to reach their nests. My guess was that few predators would follow.

Where we really racked up the life birds was the area of Brazil west of Rio de Janeiro, namely, Itatiaia National Park. We marveled at the incredibly rich bird life, such as the Green-headed Tanager [no.25] and the stunning Red-breasted Toucan [no.27]. These mountains are isolated from the rest of South America, so the endemics were everywhere. One of the most beautiful birds I have ever seen was the Black-and-Gold Cotinga, high in the mountain.

This trip brought my life list to 3385, and really turned Carol onto birding around the world. She traveled well, didn't make unrealistic demands on such a trip, and was willing to sacrifice creature comforts for the avian success of our exploits. By the end of 1988, we were already planning our next summer, which would be to the great continent of Africa.

Once we had jumped through all the administrative hoops at our respective schools the following June of 1989, we boarded a trans-Atlantic flight bound for Europe. Jet lag hit us pretty hard, but the life birds provided the no-doze effect. I now call that medicine Aviavarin. We spent a week driving around Europe from country to country, like they were states. We birded neat places described by Alden, where my two favorites were Great Reed Warblers {no.56] and Great Crested Grebe {no.57]. One night, while Carol was roaming the B&Bs of London, I camped out over the White Cliffs of Dover, was treated to a Lunar Eclipse, and listened to Elvis Presley music most of the night on one of his anniversaries.

One really interesting happenstance took place near a lake in Austria where Carol and I were looking over some waterbirds. Up the road was a snake, so naturally I tore out after it, leaving binoculars and camera rudely on the ground. I was quite excited about the snake, despite the rather bland name of "grass snake." It was, in fact, Natrix natrix, the probable ancestor of all my beloved Natricine water snakes of North America.

I stood holding the thing, and a man from the neighborhood arrived just about the time Carol got there. I began explaining all about the gentle creature in my hands, including some of its behavior. The man, whom I slightly dissed, kept trying to say something about someone from that neighborhood who knew about animal behavior, but I was too caught up in the moment to listen. Finally, he pointed to the old house near where I was standing and said the ethologist that once lived there was named (none other than) Konrad Lorenz. Boy, did I feel like a numbskull.

To the south, I thoroughly enjoyed our drive through the breathtaking Italian Alps, and discovered toads breeding in temperatures hard to imagine cold-blooded creatures being active in. Continuing on, we arrived in France, and enjoyed birding the Camargue. Seeing the hordes of flamingos was nice, but easily my favorite birds were the roller and the bee-eater. For my money, this was the top birding area of Europe, and one to which I would love to return. I must admit being shocked by some of the public behaviors of the local people, but my cosmopolitan wife helped me blow it off as local custom.

With many more lifers than expected under our belts (over 3500), we boarded a jet for Africa, on another long and exhausting flight overnight. That Aviavarin hit me at sunup, though, as we sailed in low over Nairobi National Park just before landing. I actually saw a giraffe standing out munching on an Acacia tree, but the excitement was compromised by what surely must have been Cattle Egrets.

The first day in Africa, driving through the sprawling city of Nairobi, was an experience. I liked the name of the main road, Uhurah Avenue, which I believe means "freedom" in Swahili. I didn't feel any discomfort at us being two tiny drops of milk in a very large cup of coffee, and at no time in all my travels in Africa did I feel the victim of racial prejudice or discrimination.

Our first stop, and one I would recommend for anyone visiting Kenya, was Nairobi National Park. It truly had an amazing assortment of birds, and some great stuff at that. Soon, we had recorded Ostrich, huge storks [no.49], monstrous vultures [no.60](more closely related to our eagles than New World vultures), Crowned Cranes [no.41],many herons, including the massive Goliath Heron, several raptor species, amazing little galliforms like guineas, hornbills, Superb and Blue-eared starlings [nos. 42 & 46], tiny,

Oxpecker ▶

gleaming sunbirds, an astounding array of confusing weavers, and the new love of my life, widowbirds and why-dahs. These last two have incredibly long, flowing tails attached to undersized, modest bodies.

With as much as we both enjoyed the birds, and as little as I normally pay attention to mammals, it's hard to deny that the hairy beasts stole the show. Within the first hour, we were parked by a low tree with several lions. Oh, man! During the course of the day, we drove within close proximity of several huge creatures, such as Cape Buffalo, rhino, and a very large giraffe. Many of them were carrying their very own entourage of oxpeckers, that groom insect pests off their hides.

This wonderful first day in Africa was not unlike my initial South American day, when life birds came early, often, and all day. The diversity of the African plain was staggering, and park after park just loaded our wagon with new birds, mammals and rich experiences. My favorite locations besides Nairobi were the Masai Mare Game Reserve, Amboseli National Park, Tsavo National Park,

and the coastal area around Mombasa. We saw Lesser Flamingo [no.44]and Crab Plover [no.45] near the latter location.

It was truly amazing how there wasn't a single mammal (except humans) outside the protected areas such as national parks. Even the parks were being poached in some places, and I didn't always get the feeling there was a consensus to stridently protect these natural resources. On the other hand, I am an American, and where is this more true than in our country? With all the apparent nationalist pride about their parks, it was the discovery of ecotourism that got them serious about protecting such priceless bounties of birds and mammals. And make no mistake about it, they are making a lot of money off these national parks (like up to $70/person/day).

Kenya was a wonderful country with well-run national

parks and refuges, and I would recommend this as a must stop for globe-trotting birders. We recorded 386 life birds our first two weeks alone, and many more after that. Birds are tame, so photography is easy, and there are fewer really tough complexes like antbirds and flycatchers that I faced in South America.

As nice as the African people were to us, honesty compels me to say that corruption is rampant in some places. Border guards virtually hold up tourists traveling alone for steep "fees," and other forms of bribes are common. If you take guided tours, you will be well cared for, but it's a shame we loners can't feel that same sense of safety.

Carol and I finally flew to South Africa, and headed out from Jo'berg in the Austral winter. Days were very pleasant, but nights were downright chilly. The area around Capetown represents an entirely different floral kingdom from the rest of the world, and there were correspondingly unique birds there as well. For instance, the Finbos (South Africa's unique floral kingdom) has sugarbirds, a slender group of songbird-relatives with a long tail and strongly decurved bill. There were also huge numbers of sea birds, such as a colony of cormorants, gulls and Cape Gannets [no.62].

Bontebok National Park was a favorite destination, with the namesake common and easily found. This deer-like creature, the Bontebok, is one of the truly beautiful mammals of the world, and the picture of them standing and watching us in the heavy mist of early morning has stood etched in my mind for years. Bird-wise I enjoyed the francolins and bustards a lot, but nothing made me happier than the handsome Bokmakierie. This oriole maintains

◀ Colony of Cape Gannets

much the same colors as meadowlarks, Dickcissels and several other unrelated species of grassland birds around the world, all of whom represent a textbook example of convergence. Brown back, yellow chest, black bib; have you ever seen this?

Following this, we headed north to Manna Pools, a wonderful camping area with many birds and other animals. The zoologist in me got really excited when I learned that the dried mud (we were there in the dry season) contained lung fish underneath, encased in their cocoons. I was instructed to look for the tiny holes through which they breathe, and they would not be harmed if I dug one up.

This was no easy job. I borrowed a shovel and began optimistically plunging it into the dried mud. Well, this was like concrete, and I began getting warm quickly. Not really digging, it was more like chipping away rock-hard mud, until I began to see my quarry below. I carefully dug around it, so as not to injure the fish, and finally sat proudly with this ancient creature, a close living relative to our probable tetrapod ancestor, in my possession. For a moment, though, I wondered if this triumphant unearthing was to be my last act on earth.

I stood up, glanced over the edge of the depression in which I was standing, and found myself face to face with a lion. She couldn't have been more than twenty feet away, and I was wondering if I was going to be called on to use my shovel for a purpose other than its intended one (the pun that she might not want to be "spayed" crossed my mind, but only weak smile creased my face). I then decided if I was on the way out, I'd die as casually as I'd lived. I spoke up, looking right at her, and said, "I hope you've given up red meat." Then I slowly turned and walked away, living to fight another day. Whew!

That evening, feeling pretty good about the lung fish (which I'd released into a small pond) and just being alive, I said what must have been the all-time dumbest thing I've ever said. Carol and I were eating some delicacy like sardines for supper, and a panicked woman came into camp, babbling about her son just having cut his hand. She was looking for a physician to sew him up, and she asked if I was a doctor. I looked at her with complete straight-forwardness, and said, "No, but I am a taxidermist." Carol nearly died.

My experience with cats, which I've never been overly fond of, continued at our next destination. We drove up to the Namibian Desert and saw more weaver finches than I ever care to again. There were also several eagle species and many terrestrial birds running hither and yon. But at one juncture, we were stopped by some folks who gave us directions to a leopard. Problem was, they neglected to say it was in a tree.

We drove up and down that road until our tires fell off, and we didn't see it. Finally, as we were giving up and driving off, Carol glanced up in an acacia tree (where we should have been looking all along) and there it was. It was a bulky cat, with beautiful colors and typical lazy, cat eyes. I was very impressed by it, and got out to get a good picture. Suddenly, as it stood and started slowly down the limb, I realized that creature could be on me before I could say "oh heck," and I snapped the shot and got back in. Intellectually, I know that neither leopards nor lions make a practice of attacking people, but try telling yourself that when those yellow eyes are fixed on you, and they lick their lips.

It is curious that the roll of film in my camera was ruined in development, and that one shot – the last on the roll – was the only one that came out. It was the Leopard.

On the way back from Leopard Lane, my life list had reached 3999, and I was on the prowl for the next-to-last milestone. Something within me said to watch the raptors, and there were certainly several I had not yet recorded. My instincts were correct, but you know how that is – we remember the 10% of the time we predict correctly, and forget the other 90%. At any rate, while wheeling over a rise, a good-sized, all-brown form sailed across my field of view, and I bolted out to try a picture of this creature. It was a Brown Snake-Eagle, triumphant life bird number 4000.

Our trip continued after many weeks on the road with a visit to Kruger National Park, at the other end of the rift valley in South Africa. That is a huge, national treasure, well run and full of wildlife. We also visited many places

in-between, and life birds continued to come furiously. We really hadn't been to west Africa, though, and I looked forward to our final destinations — Victoria Falls and Zaire.

The Victoria Falls area was loaded with more new birds, and the forests that drink deeply from the mist are rich in all life. One day at the falls, Carol wanted to work the trees, and I wanted to snake hunt around the water. As I was returning in about an hour, some guy came hurriedly down the trail, and instructed me to beware of an angry elephant. He said that some lady had tried singing to one, and it made an angry charge at her. I asked if she was wearing a turquoise shirt, and the blank stare on his face assured me that elephants had the same taste in music as humans.

Carol bounced back fine from the musical spurn, and we birded Zimbabwe and Zambia for several days. We could feel ourselves tiring somewhat, from modest food and often difficult sleeping conditions. One night, the bells from the stupid cows kept clanging all night long, and we struggled to stay the course the next day. Clearly, we need-ed to go home to our classrooms and crash.

Last on the agenda, we birded like crazy around Kinshasa, and then drove north to the Congo River. From there, we headed inland, and birded all patches of tropical forest along the way. Carol and I became especially close that last week, and what we had accomplished together made us proud as well. Our best find was a nesting Batis flycatcher, the genus of which supposedly didn't occur in this region. This became somewhat of a tense situation, as it unfolded.

◀ *Batis Flycatcher*

Naturally, I wanted to get a reasonable picture of this bird on her nest, as it apparently represented a record of some import. I popped out of the car and took several angles of it, paying no attention to a jeep roaring toward us from a building set back from the road. Actually, it was a military installation.

Two very large men with really large guns got out and demanded to know what I was doing. I didn't mind explaining, but then they demanded my film. I told them it was a picture of a bird, but of course when they asked, I couldn't show them the bird in the book, because it wasn't in the book. Oh, man. I just decided they wouldn't risk an international incident, so to their astonishment, I thanked them for their concern and started walking toward the car. However, I kept my eye on Carol, knowing that if one of them raised a gun, she'd alter her behavior considerably. Well, she didn't, they didn't, and I didn't. The framed picture of that little Batis sits in my livingroom, as further proof that I am totally insane.

Having escaped Africa with our lives and roughly a thousand life birds, we probably should have quit while we were ahead. However, due to our desire to see Serenghetti National Park, we returned not long after our first visit. The plan was to purchase a car in Nairobi and drive into Tanzania. We had trouble finding a decent car, but settled on a used Mercedes that seemed in good condition. It was a tough car, had plenty of room for us both to sleep on a seat if need be, and got good mileage.

The trip started uneventfully enough, with short trips to Nairobi National Park and several other refuges of which I had learned. Then, it was time to cross into Tanzania, and head for the great Serenghetti National Park. One stop that was one of those "remove your shoes" kind of holy ground places was Olduvai Gorge, where Dr. Leaky made such profound advancements in our understanding of human origins. Places like that, the house of Konrad Lorenz, or the Charles Darwin Research Station evokes such intellectual emotion to those of us who appreciate the cornerstones of science, and the price that was paid for these foundations.

Continuing on, we came to Lion Hill, where huge numbers of the King of Beasts hang out, waiting for supper to come to them. Apparently, this is on a straight line between the ungulate's feeding area and the only water source, so the crafty lions know they'll be comin'. We had actually passed thousands of gazelles and antelope not far back, so we were running the same gauntlet they have to run. These wonderful, well-fed cats just lay there, hardly showing a care in the world, and lazily put on a great show as we tooled on past.

Serenghetti National Park was everything it was cracked up to be, and more. We saw the Wildebeest migration, and it was an almost continuous river of mammals as far as we could see. Carol especially got off on things like that, and I must say it was an awesome sight. Several days around the park brought us good birds, but we were mammal-watchers as much as anything. My favorite of those was a small group of Cheetahs, so sleek, and fast as greased lightning.

We saw surprisingly few snakes in Africa, although some night driving did bring me a python, Puff Adder (a deadly African snake), and some harmless colubrids. One night we also drove up behind two male lions ambling down the road, presumably unable to capture a pride of their own.

My high school had the lion as their mascot (typical of schools to choose animals that occur half way around the world), so I took some "pride" in their majesty. The shame that this creature was possibly the laziest animal on earth was only mitigated by the fact that males are capable of mating every fifteen minutes. No wonder they call them the King of Beasts.

As we left Serenghetti National Park, we began having a series of car problems. First, we tried crossing a large, rocky mud puddle, and got stuck in the middle of it. Then, while trying to get it unstuck, I realized the fuel line had come apart. Gas was streaming out into the puddle, and we didn't have a lot to spare to get back across the border to Kenya. I frantically jacked up the heavy car and half swam, half crawled under the car to repair the line. The jack was perched on a smooth rock, and I knew it could have fallen at any minute. I was scared, cold and wet, and now very worried about whether we had fuel to get out of nowhere. Finally, I fixed the line, put some of those nasty rocks under the tires, and drove that sucker out of the quagmire.

The second car problem occurred two hours later. The ruts were getting deeper in the road, and we began hitting bottom a few times. I was concerned that we would tear the fuel line again, but at least it wouldn't be a secret, since it quickly cuts the car off. Finally, after some moves that would make any halfback proud, I goofed and landed unceremoniously on the middle ridge. We were stuck, and the left wheels were off the ground. Oh, man.

Once again out of the car (not recommended for Africa), I began working on getting us unstuck. It was tough with no really large rocks or boards, and the jack barely lifted that Mercedes. All the while I was working, though, a lion sat out on the hill watching me. It seemed that every time I looked around, he was a tad closer. I finally couldn't continue lying there working with my back to him; something had to be done.

I pitched semi-pro baseball until I was 30, so I had a decent enough arm. I picked up a fist-sized rock, and fired it toward the lion. I was so nervous, I under threw him by a country mile, and the rock skipped harmlessly to a halt. Gathering myself, I tried again, but the rock sailed way over the lion's position, and he barely gave it a glance. Changing strategy, I tried throwing the third high in the air, and letting it drop near enough to spook him away.

This rock was nearly the size of a softball, and it took my best heave to get it up and over his spot. But to my utter amazement, that rock came down right on his head, and bounced high in the air. It truly is a wonder and a miracle it didn't kill him. He snarled angrily, rose straight up in the air, and turned his King of Beast tail and ran like a scalded dog, all the time shaking his head and mane. I really felt awful that I'd hit that dumb animal, but what were the odds?

We finally got going, and spent the night among the jackals and hyenas. Carol slept in the car, which all sane people would do, but I stretched out in the tent, after having a pretty "in tents" day as well. It was a wonderful feeling hearing all the sounds of Africa, many of which one hears on nature shows. But to actually be out among them

— now that was exciting. I heard lions way off in the distance, but I figured they all heard the sky was falling in my area.

The next day we were to arrive back in Kenya, but we had another car issue to deal with. As we were tooling down the sorry, dirt road, the car suddenly stopped dead. It wouldn't crank, but still had barely enough gas to get us back. It was firing, and I finally concluded it was the fuel pump. Oh, man, what could I do? We hadn't seen another car in two days, and there were few options.

I decided to get fancy, and try a jury rig. I removed the squirter dealie from the windshield wiper assembly and mounted it on top of the car. I then ran its hose down into the fuel injectors, and filled the plastic container with syphoned gas (I hate doing that). Eureka! It worked! Off we went for about 16 miles, until I had to fill it again. After several refills, we reached the Tanzania border, where we had to bribe our way back into Kenya.

Having fixed the fuel pump, we headed into the Masai Mare Game Preserve to enjoy a great area for birds. The road there, however, had a hundred yards that is the worst section of road I have ever seen in the world! It goes steeply uphill, and has monster boulders sticking out of the ground that just eats cars with limited clearance. It is a miracle in itself that we got to the top, but what was left of the left front was pretty much junk. We figured that's the way the Mercedes bends.

Somehow we made our way to the mechanical unit of the reserve and they pulled and pushed the various metal pieces into some semblance of shape. It now was operational, but had a terminal case of the ker-plunks. It was too bad two school teachers couldn't have afforded an SUV, but we had done the best we could with what we had. We reward our students for that, so we weren't going to beat ourselves up too much.

We flew to Cairo, Egypt as we left Kenya, and spent several days birding the desert. The mornings were cool, but it was amazing how hot it got by noon. There were a few really neat birds out on the Sahara, though, and watching their behavior was really interesting.

We also did a day of tourism, where we went to the Sphinx and pyramids. What the heck. Carol really gave me a good laugh when a man offered to help her up on a camel for free so she could get a picture, and then charged her five dollars to help her down. She came walking up sheepishly and said, "He gypped me" (like E - gypt). You had to have been there.

This was the only bad birding trip I ever took, and must confess regretting it somewhat. The second Africa trip's financial cost was enormous, and we had so little to show for many thousands of dollars. At the risk of belaboring the joke, we both felt a little gypped, and might be hesitant to return to Africa. I must admit that Africa is the best continent for bird photography, as they are big, tame, and sit out in the open. Several I especially liked were the Red-billed Hornbill [no.47], Ground Hornbill [no.48], Long-tailed and Fiscal Shrikes [nos.58 & 61], and the Martial Eagle [no. 63].

CHAPTER SEVEN

COMING CLOSE IN ASIA

For three years following the big African trip, I went on a lot of shorter trips, attempting to fill in some gaps in my life list. Lovely places Carol and I visited included some Caribbean locations, another trip to South America, western Alaska, Arizona in winter, the Dry Tortugas, Eastern Canada and many more. I also took a wonderful excursion to Trinidad and Tobago with Richard Perry, the best friend I have ever known. Richard taught biology with me at Leon, and in my darkest hour, which was to come, he would stand with me unconditionally.

In 1991, I took the entire summer and treated several kids to "The Western Trip," where we loaded up a van and went to Arizona, the Rockies, the Sierras and The West Coast up to Washington. I had several target birds which I selfishly arranged to see, but the kids had the time of their lives. Having students who eventually pursued biology in college and for a career was very important to me, and this type of adventure seemed to spur some on deeper into science.

My life list stood at 4311, and I tried to keep track on the trip as best I could. On our first stop in Arizona, Rufous-winged Sparrow brought me one notch higher, and we all took the long walk through the canyon for snakes, and my Five-striped Sparrow. At this point, I was beginning to wonder what new bird I could even get here, but it was time to head west.

We road cruised on the west Arizona desert that night for snakes, finding Glossy Snakes, Long-nosed Snakes, Sidewinder and a little Leaf-nosed Snake. Also, though, right in the lights of our van, and sitting on a Saguaro Cactus, sat my earlier nemesis, the Elf Owl. I couldn't believe how small it was, and it just sat there, blinking at us. I can't honestly say that the past two years held the same excitement over life birds as earlier in my life, but the excitement of this bird was inspiring. I told them I just wanted one more life bird that summer, and they assured me I'd get it.

Off we went to the West Coast, and we just began having a great time. The national parks of the Sierras were grand and beautiful, and my students soaked up information like a sponge. Two weeks went by without a life bird, but that wasn't a problem. It was a fun trip for all, a very educational one as well, and I found myself relaxing like few trips in my life. Oddly, it seemed the pressure to reach goals and see new birds may have been robbing me of the trip's joy.

Toward the end of the trip, we arrived in Washington and headed for Olympic National Park. I had told the stu-

dents about salamandering in this area, and we began finding several exciting species within the first few minutes.
One kid really had a hard time with the fact that they neither had lungs nor gills. The whole experience helped
them to see the value of the old growth forests, though,
and they had a hard time understanding why a nation
would utterly destroy such a marvelous ecosystem. Greed
is a disease that often doesn't come of age until the adult
years.

Then, so very unexpectedly, it happened. I had been
checking out a flock of chickadees, looking for one of
those beautiful Pacific northwest warblers (just to admire
them), and lo and behold, there was my long-desired life
bird, sitting right out on a limb, like he didn't give a
"hoot." It was a Spotted Owl — the very bird I had been
telling my students about! I stood countless moments just
staring at this creature, wondering how anyone could
completely take his home away. Then, I took a very long,
deep breath, and felt satisfied with my bird list on the trip.

Still, later while driving out to Cape Flattery, I found
myself more excited about having shown this bird to my
students than I was about adding it to my life list. This
was an important moment for me, as for the first time, I
questioned my resolve to go the final course. I so loved
teaching and working with tomorrow's future, I wondered
if I would make seeing nearly another thousand life birds
a high enough priority to invest that time and money.

The rest of the trip went well; I added Chukar to my life
list, and we returned home safely after six weeks on the
road. Carol and I had a long talk about trips, and we
agreed to go to Asia the following summer. There was

much she wanted to see in that area of the world, and I felt duty-bound to complete my quest for five thousand life birds. Little did I know it would nearly claim my life.

On June 5, 1992, we drove out to California and boarded the big bird for Japan. The birding was fair, but this part of the trip was expensive. The Japanese people were very friendly and efficient, but I had never been in a place where there was so little diversity in a population's appearance. They were eager to welcome us everywhere we went, but I'm just glad I didn't have to learn individual names!

The lowlands had virtually all been converted to rice fields, and there were some interesting birds there. Kingfishers especially were lovely birds, and many of the wading birds were striking and different from my past experiences. It was curious to me that the ibis that many consider to be the National Bird of Japan, which was shown on the field guide, was extinct in this country (of course, for years, the Brown Pelican was extirpated from Louisiana, where it is the state bird).

Some of the woodlands were in better shape, owing to the difficulty of farming mountains (a common thread around the world). There were a number of fascinating corvids, quite an array of buntings, and some majestic fly-catchers. But the most interesting experience was hearing a double note near a forest clearing that I knew I should recognize. It was a mellow, whistled pair of notes, with the second a major third below the first. While my mind was up in the clouds somewhere, my wife looked at me with an inquisitive face, and asked if that wasn't a cuckoo. Ah, sooo!

There weren't loads of insectivorous birds on the islands

of Japan, despite the summer season. In fact, the entire time we were there, not one bug hit the windshield! Have the people so completely bombed their environment with pesticides that the bugs are gone? I don't know, and can only speculate, but I didn't miss cleaning the windshield.

China is a massive country with hordes of people and disappearing natural areas. My favorite part of China was Taiwan, a beautiful, mountainous island with lush rain forests and some spectacular scenery. We arrived in the smog of Taipei, where many in the city wear masks to guard against the air pollution. Soon, we were in our rented car and headed around the north end of the island to the eastern forests. We were not at all crowded, and enjoyed several days of lovely birding.

While we were there, I had the strangest experience. Carol and I were parked up in the mountains eating lunch, and I noticed a frog, not unlike the leopard frogs of America, moving in the leaves outside the driver's window. It jumped and landed head-first, a rather odd behavior for a frog. It tried to lurch again, and landed on its side. I continued to watch it, and it finally lay still.

This required some investigating. I hopped out and found the frog stone dead! I combed the leaves and grass for predators, and there were none. For his part, the frog had some of his entrails hanging out of his side, but from what? I took pictures of this, and detailed notes, but came to no conclusions. Back home that fall, I contacted some Chinese herpetologists, and they had no idea what caused this to happen. I swear, for the life of me, I will never know what killed that frog, and made his intestines eek out.

Our visit to the eastern edge of Taiwan was wonderful, with many birds and breathtaking vistas. There are some deeply wooded canyons that wind their way back from the ocean's shoreline, which were as beautiful as any on earth. In some places, the road actually went well under the mountain, creating some of the most beautiful highway miles anywhere. Finding good patches to bird away from traffic wasn't easy, but eventually we found most of what there was to see.

As if the frog experience wasn't weird enough, there was more excitement after dark one evening. We were road cruising for snakes and having some luck, when I stopped for a colorful serpent about eighteen inches long. In the headlights, I pinned his head down carefully, as for all I knew, it could have been some deadly elapid. I secured it with my left hand, which I always use picking up poisonous snakes, and started back to the car to plop the creature in a snake bag. Then, to my horror, I suddenly felt a sharp pain in my left hand, while the snake was wrapped around it.

Folks, you cannot, in your wildest dreams, imagine my reaction. Hollering some choice words (I hope it wasn't too bad), I flung that snake off my hand and over the mountainside, no doubt picking up more G's than a snake ever knew (I cannot imagine poor Carol's reaction at this point, nor what was going through the snake's small mind). I placed my hand in front of the headlight, and examined the offended spot. There was only one small indentation between my thumb and forefinger, and any pain I felt had already subsided.

Taiwan mountain ▶

It was now clear to me what had happened: The snake was one of the barb-tailed species (like the Mud Snake of North America) which stick their pointed tail into any animal that picks them up. There was absolutely no danger to me at all, and I felt pretty stupid having reacted in such an extreme way. Obviously, being a human being wasn't reason enough.

Our next destination was Bangkok, Thailand, where we hoped to see many great birds, and did. We left the unattractive city and headed northeast to Khao Yai National Park. The drive along the way grew better and better for birds. Best of all were the rice patties, which were loaded with all kinds of shorebirds, waders and offbeat aquatic species. Notable species include the lovely Cinnamon Bittern, graceful Pied Harriers, White-breasted Waterhens sneaking around, and the massive Great Hornbill as we entered the park. Birds were tame, pho-

tography was easy, and I really began enjoying the quest for 5000 species once again.

We overnighted near the south edge of the great national park, and road cruised for snakes down old country roads that paralleled rice fields. We were doing pretty well, including having my first look at a Sunbeam Snake (a new family of snakes!), when I noticed a plump, dark snake on the roadside, about twenty inches long. I couldn't locate the flashlight, and knew the snake was likely to get away, so I hopped out and gently pinned it down with my boot.

Carol came over with a light after securing the car (never an important priority to me), and when I shined the light on the snake, I just gasped. It was a Russell's Viper! This creature has the most deadly venom outside Australia, and the smallest amount would be more than enough to take me out. Worse, they have a nerve gas that is released from their venom when they bite, and it was doing a very professional job on my boot at the moment. Sure enough, I

White-breasted Waterhen

began to feel weak and faint, undoubtedly the effects of the gas.

This was great! I was actually experiencing the results of a Russell's Viper, and I was going to live to tell about it. I waited until my head cleared, held my breath and very carefully pinned down the head and dropped him in a snake bag — bound for the trunk. The next day, I took great pictures of him, but this night was a special one, indeed.

The next day we entered Khao Yai National Park, and the birds were everywhere! Unlike the marsh birds in the rice patties, these were almost all new. We saw diversities of green-pigeons, cuckoos, a lovely trogon, several barbets and handsome woodpeckers, warblers, flycatchers, sunbirds and several kingfishers along the watercourses. My favorite birds were the leafbirds, who are green as a gourd and well-named for sure. I passed 4500 life birds that afternoon, but am disappointed that I do not know which bird it was. It may have been the lovely Magpie Robin.

▼ *Magpie Robin*

That night, Carol and I camped in the most wilderness area we could find, and really had quite a scare. We both woke up in a start, as the bellows of a tiger roared through our campsite. Once again, I knew intellectually that these great cats — actually larger than lions — generally leave people alone. But because we are human, it was a little unsettling to hear this beast out there in the dark of the night. Over the next several nights, we got used to him, and I just learned to pretend it was Carol snoring.

We really mopped up the life birds in Khao Yai, but finally had to say farewell. On the way out of the park, though, I had one of the great snake experiences of my life. Along with my now fulfilled desire to catch an anaconda, I always wanted to catch a cobra, preferably a King Cobra. The fact that they were huge, smart and quick didn't deter me; I wanted to hang one on my mind's wall in the worst way.

On the way down the hill, leaving the park, I got my chance. The huge but slender form of a tan brown snake was easing off the left side of the road, heading off into the veld. I had traded my boots and jeans for shorts and moccasins, but I was not going to be denied. I came to a screeching halt, grabbed my bamboo stick, and dashed out into the grass like a complete idiot.

Had it continued with coachwhip speed, never to be seen again? My gut didn't think so, although there was a part of me that hoped it did. This was very dangerous! Seconds later, I heard him rustle slightly, and thought, "Move toward him." I was really scared, for I knew about these creatures by reputation. They had a way of winning their confrontations, and I didn't especially want to be their next victim.

Mustering all the courage I had, I stepped slightly forward, and what happened next was perhaps the most chilling experience of my life. A few feet in front of me, I saw the great snake's massive head about four feet off the ground. Then, to my amazement, it was even with my head! Finally, in an act that left me astonished and actually shaking, I realized I was looking up at the monster's head. He was so long that the head was seven feet off the ground. Discretion being the better part of valor, I backed away slowly, keeping one eye on the devil's head. I knew if it came at me I could kill it with the bat-like bamboo I had, but killing it was the second-worst option I could think of. Having both of us escape unscathed but uncaptured was the second-best, but would have to do.

I drove off, slowly at first, without either of us saying a word. We were all the way out of the park, a good fifteen minutes later, when Carol finally said in a soft voice, "Good move."

We birded some other areas of Thailand, such as along the coast, and saw quite a few new birds there. I also caught my first cobra, a Monocled Cobra, and spent a day snorkeling the South China Sea. We had a great time watching cuttlefish swim along the reefs, changing color to match whatever they were swimming past. I also saw a couple of sea snakes, but being underwater and defenseless, I decided to give them a break

What I did take from that day was by far the worst sunburn I have ever had. I kid you not, I peeled twice before it was all over. The next day, I could hardly sit in the car, and life birds were a rather low priority for several days. Still, we worked hard, pushing our life bird total to 400 for the summer.

The western extent of our Thailand travels took us to the Burma border, well up in the mountains, where it practically rained life birds. I also caught a Slug-eating Snake, a creature whose name says it all. This was a beautiful section of Thailand, and a place I would love to return one day. The name of the location was Doi Inthanon National Park, and it was among the most beautiful places I've visited on earth, with the rich montane flavor.

Doi Inthanon had loads of new birds, some practically endemic, with gaudy sunbirds so tame I could almost touch them. Still, my favorite bird was a Peregrine Falcon. I always like to see Peregrines, but this marked the fifth (!) continent on which I've seen that species. Some birds such as Barn Owls and Black-crowned Night-Herons just seem to get around, and I guess the Peregrine does as easily as anyone (yes, I know there's a much better scientific explanation).

Our next destination was Taman Negara National Park in Malaysia. It is mostly hilly to mountainous rain forest, and much of it is really wilderness. We stayed in some cabins overlooking a cliff, and spent some time boating on the Tembeling River. Moving around the way we did allowed us to see many new birds over a span of a few weeks, and this park was no exception.

Early on the trip I heard a scream that I did not recognize, but doubted it was avian. That hunch proved true, as I found one in the high canopy, and it was a wonderful

White-handed Gibbon. There are four great apes in the world: gorillas, chimpanzees, gibbons and Orangutan. Were I listing such creatures, I could have now claimed three out of four. Little did I know that I might not live to see the fourth.

Some of the really neat birds we saw in the park included the huge Rhinoceros Hornbill, drongos, many bulbuls and babblers, pitas, three hawk-eagles (!), and my first honeyguide. For my money, though, the bird of the trip was the Green Broadbill. This velvet-looking little emerald just melted my heart, and made me wonder how I could be so lucky as to travel the world looking at birds.

We really mopped up the life birds, but it was time to head for Kuala Lumpur. We barely made our flight to Singapore, and kept reminding ourselves that they had very strict enforcement of laws in this tiny country. I have never used drugs, but receiving the death penalty for smoking pot seems a bit harsh. It was sure worth coming to Singapore, though, as there were many varied bird species in the Bukit Timah Nature Reserve.

I loved the rather common Brahminy Kites[no.21] that floated along the seashore, and recorded my first Cinnamon Heron in a small marsh as well — life bird number 4570! Others that really grabbed my attention were the wagtails, Pied Fantail, White-throated Kingfisher [no.52], Large Woodshrike and the beautiful Black-naped Oriole. It just blew me away that there were so many new birds everywhere I went.

I really had wanted to visit the small island where Komodo Dragons (those huge lizards that eat toilets) could be seen, but we only had ten weeks. We flew instead to the Malaysian country of Borneo, where there were some good patches of forest, and the beautiful Kinabalu National Park.

What we found almost immediately were cobras seemingly everywhere. Regrettably, one of them had my name on its fangs, and that first night in Borneo nearly became my last night on earth.

We birded some orchards in the afternoon, and it was really hot. We had managed to stay in the mountains most of the trip, but this area was low and muggy. The birding wasn't great that afternoon, and we camped early in a grove of fruiting trees. We had a nice jeep with a good a/c, and used it quite a lot that day, as well as early evening.

We crawled into the tent around nine, both dressed in shorts and a T-shirt, using no cover. It was stifling hot and hard to sleep. Somewhere around midnight, Carol had to run outside (she always drank so much water!). As she opened the tent door, I watched her through my bleary eyes. She was being pretty careful, as I warned her several times about the snakes, but accidents do happen.

In a moment of terror, I saw a cobra rise up right by my wife's left leg, and I knew it could end her life. Simply out of instinct, I lunged at the snake from my prone position, and hit the snake right in the head. Immediately, I grabbed the flashlight from Carol, and beat the heck out of the dazed reptile. Tragedy averted, right?

Well, not exactly. Carol was pretty upset, so I just held her for a few moments. She really handled most situations very well, and one could hardly blame her for being upset. Unfortunately, as my hand was wrapped around her back, I couldn't seem to feel anything in my pinky. I changed my position, hoping it had just gone to sleep. Several minutes later, two fingers were numb, so I picked up the beleaguered flashlight and felt my heart sink as two fang marks appeared on my smallest finger. I had been bitten by a cobra, and there was virtually nothing I could do.

Breaking the news to Carol didn't help her emotional state much, and she was smart enough to know that people usually died from cobra bites. We had a short discussion about going to a far-off hospital, but I knew I was allergic to horse serum, so I was probably allergic to the pig serum of Asia. It was fourth and long, and might be time to punt.

Maybe not. I remembered two herpetologists (OK, they were just snake hunters) telling me that some folks in Colombia use stun guns to neutralize venom in fresh snake-bite cases. The electricity in spark plug wires was similar in some ways to stun guns, so I bounced out of the tent and cranked up the jeep. I pulled off the number 2 spark plug wire and stuck it on the bite area, and my friends, I have never felt so much pain in my life. This venom had been killing nerves and causing anything but pain, but I found out quickly that there were many healthy nerves in there as well. I applied the wires as many times as I could stand it, and I was literally shaking in pain. I guess you could say I would be shocked if I lived from this electrifying experience, as cobra bites were usually terminal. Real funny.

Following this self-torture, I got in the jeep with Carol, turned on the a/c with the motor running, and promised her I was going to live. Of course, I knew if I broke that promise, I wouldn't have to listen to her yell at me about it. Intellectually, I knew I should suffocate within two hours, but in my heart, I honestly felt I was going to survive.

In the short time ahead, I began having trouble breathing, although the car's a/c did help in that regard. Plus, I never wanted to die hot and uncomfortable. While I dozed, I saw the most vivid colors, wild images and all sorts of hallucinations. It seemed that I had been asleep for several hours, and hoped against hope that I had turned the corner. Then I really slept deeply.

As the first rays of the sun crept over the horizon, and I made out the shape of the limbs and leaves, it "dawned" on me that I would live to bird another day. Carol was sound asleep, as I know she was up a lot during the night. Bless her heart. I started to run my hand through my balding pate, as I so often do early in the morning, and the message didn't get to my right arm. Ooops. I tested my muscles down my right side, and there was only a sporadic response. My nervous system was cooked. But hey, I was breathing, I was going to live, and there was a bulbul right outside calling his little pea-picking head off. Time to go!

Carol woke up and we celebrated my continued existence briefly, but we both heard nature's still small voice. With both of us watching pretty darn carefully where we were stepping, we found relief without sacrificing safety. I hobbled back to the jeep, not attaining much feeling in my right leg. Two granola bars later, we were on our way to the orangutan preserve, and the atmosphere in our jeep was fairly subdued.

Limping along the trails, we actually recorded plenty of life birds, and finally came face to face with a sure-fire orangutan (my fourth and last great ape, our nearest cousin). It really was a beautiful creature, with an orange hue and a remarkably human face. They have learned to trust people in this protected confine, so my camera spoke repeatedly. I must say, they look better in the wild than in zoos.

The next day, we began working Mount Kinabalu, the highest peak between the Himalayas and New Guinea. Life birds were so easy on this isolated island, and some remarkably beautiful birds were easily found. Some I especially loved were Black-and-crimson Oriole, Wreathed Hornbill, Red-bearded Bee-eater (lower down), Lesser Coucal (what a splendid bird!), the Large Hawk-Cuckoo, two very colorful barbets, several babblers, jungle-flycatchers, and two flowerpeckers.

We really found more birds in the lowlands, and seem to discover life birds in bunches. There was a dull pain in my right leg, and at times I just had to sit down or collapse. I also knew that Carol was feeling some of that Catholic guilt, so I tried to hide the creeping pain. I have found through the years that people will release their guilt when they are ready, and there is nothing others can generally do about it. Still, it wasn't her fault.

We finished by heading into the foothills of central Borneo, once again finding more life birds just jumping out of the woods. The western part of the island didn't interest me, and time was now running short. I knew I was at 4832, and wondered optimistically if I would reach the magical goal of 5000 on this trip. Up next, last but not least, the Philippines.

We took Alden's advice, and concentrated our efforts on

three large islands. I could have done without the drive through Manila, an extremely large, tedious city which takes forever to cross. I was beginning to get the "bottom of the ninth" syndrome, where I felt pressure to bust my rear end at the end of the trip. I must say, we did work pretty hard.

Three hours from Manila, Quezon National Park was incredibly beautiful, and loaded with birds. I marveled at how wide-ranging trogons were, salivated over a Fairy Bluebird, and recorded the bird of the trip, a Great Philippine Eagle. This magnificent creature reminded me of a Harpy Eagle, though perhaps more slender. They aren't as powerful as the New World species (harpy), but if you're a Crab-eating Macaque, you better know they aren't monkeying around, either.

We birded all over Luzon, and not only added many lifers, we saw an incredible array of neat birds. There were Blue-tailed Bee-eaters, Green Racquet-tail, the lovely Bleeding-heart Pigeon (so common in American zoos), Tarictic Hornbill and one lovely Philippine Falconet.

On to Mindanao, we visited Mt. Apo, though the road was bad and it was tough getting into decent forests. We still saw 38 more lifers, and again, some sensational birds like Fire-breasted Flowerpecker, Naked-faced Spider-hunter (life bird number 4900) and Scarlet Minivet. I keep thinking of the jokes I could make from some of these names.

The somewhat isolated island of Palawan stood as our last destination, and offered many unique and interesting birds. Finding the holder of my second-favorite bird name, the Andalusian Hemipode, was a top priority, and it only came with a lot of searching. Still aching from my cobra rendezvous, I walked with both pain and purpose. We also saw the Palawan Peacock-Pheasant, the handsome but odd Stork-billed Kingfisher, and the lovely Blue Paradise-Flycatcher.

We couldn't resist the boat trip out to Tabon Island, where there are more megapodes than pigs in Arkansas. The birding was good, but I thoroughly enjoyed the relaxation in front of the crystal-clear water, and the invertebrate life on the low-tide flats. Favorites out here were the hairy brittlestars, huge and detailed. Interestingly, I felt my stress level falling, as I knew I had done everything I could do to reach the impossible dream of 5000 birds. We returned to the United States with my life list 4972, and I was totally satisfied with our Asian trip.

On the day before our flight back to the states, we hopped the small boat for mainland Palawan. It was to be a simple trip, maybe a half-hour or so. There didn't need to be anything dangerous or exciting. Carol was exhausted, and the boat captain never wants excitement. Too bad I always have to come along and ruin the peace.

My GOD! There was a Blue-banded Sea Snake! I muttered "Hydrophis ceruleansis" to the captain and hopped overboard into the drink. No psychoanalysis, no deep-rooted meaning about a death wish, and don't ever question my maturity. I've just always wanted to hold a sea snake, and this species was as beautiful as they come. I secured the flat-tailed serpent, made my way to the shallows, and Carol took a decent picture.

Now, I could go home.

▲ *Jim with Blue-banded Sea Snake*

CHAPTER EIGHT

PASSAGE TO PARADISE

Returning to my high school job at my Alma Mater, I found myself more and more deeply engrossed in all aspects of work. I taught an overload, spent many weekends camping with my students conducting their infield research projects, and I became even more involved in the running of the school through faculty positions. I was willingly owned — lock, stock and barrel — by Leon High School, with birds and marriage taking a back seat.

I loved the work with my students, who needed their head examined for taking electives with such a demanding teacher as myself. I taught upper-level, college-prep courses such as zoology, marine biology and ecology (all honors-level), in addition to honors and gifted biology for poor underclassmen who had no choice. We had a family within the classroom, especially the fifteen or so officers of the three science clubs I sponsored. I dearly loved my "kids," and am fairly certain they satisfied any paternal instincts I may have otherwise had.

For her part, Carol also had no desire for kids of her own. She was also deeply involved with programs such as soccer and drama at her school, and no doubt touched the lives of many kids every day. In addition, she spent a fair amount of time with her nieces, which gave this Italian woman her "family" strokes. It was probably a good thing we had the common interest of traveling for birds, as we tended to drift apart in our separate worlds during the academic year.

Carol had the wonderful ability, though, to ignore the stupidity of certain aspects of her school, or maybe just vent and forget them. I couldn't. It deeply bothered me that the true welfare of the students was so often lost because of self-seeking politicians masquerading as "educators." Kids were punished for lying, yet school officials constantly painted pictures for us as far removed from truth and reality as Pluto is from Mercury. The only way I survived was to shut my classroom door and try to imagine that school was no more than a group of motivated students. Still, the damage was taking its toll on me, and it was only a matter of time before it got the best of me.

The year took a tough turn when my father died after school on November 4, 1991. I played the strong role, showing no emotion and giving the eulogy at the funeral. Knowing work to be medicinal, I even taught the next day, with my favorite lecture (the rise of vertebrates) already scheduled. Far tougher was having to proof his monumental book, with all those bird records from the past, each with heart-wrenching silent stories attached. Still, I doubt it would have ever been published had it not been for the co-author, Bruce Anderson. Our family, and me especially, owe Bruce far more than I can ever say in these sentences.

Surviving this difficult year, Carol and I headed for the birding bonanza of South America once again. This trip was different, though, as I wanted to share Peru with my wife, and just relax. We retraced many of my former tracks, and frankly, I didn't add many life birds. She really enjoyed Machu Picchu, and Abra Malaga Pass was everything I had promised. I wasn't bored at all by the inability to secure many life birds, and drew great pleasure from playing tour guide for my wife.

A number of things occurred to me on this trip. One was just how tightly wrapped I became by year's end in my teaching position. I must have been difficult to live with! A second was how much I enjoy showing others birds. It wasn't just because it was my wife; I felt many of the same things on the Western Trip with my students. It is a wonderful world, loaded with all kinds of animalian blessings. I truly grooved on watching the awe in the eyes of others when shown a majestic hawk or a Giant Hummingbird. In the classroom, I could only take kids so far, but this was the real thing! I could get used to this.

The summer was painfully short, and it was time to return to the land of paperwork and hassles. My classes and clubs grew each year in quality and participation, but it was never the kids that wore on me. The parents were great, too, and served my classroom with a support group that I was learning to rely and lean on for all kinds of help. They wanted me there, and that meant a lot.

The year took on the same dichotomy of feeling great when I was with the students, but feeling frustration with the administration and ambivalence at home. The drive from our house on the coast, situated inside a National Wildlife Refuge, wore me out, what with dodging the dump truck brigade, and fussing at slow Wakulla County residents who need to stay off the road during rush hour traffic. Increasingly, I found myself in no frame of mind to face the front office at 7:00 a.m.

A short break in the school year occurred when Carol and I celebrated our five-year anniversary by flying to the Dry Tortugas in early May. We camped and relaxed in the paradise of no bugs, lots of birds, easily-caught Red Snapper, coral reefs to snorkel, and pleasant temperatures. Other than the regular songbirds migrants, we had a bonanza of good records, including La Sagra's Flycatcher, White-tailed Tropicbird, Shiny Cowbird, Antillean Nighthawk, Couch's Kingbird and Black Noddy. We even saw a Merlin feeding on the buffet, and a Cattle Egret eating exhausted Barn Swallows. Of course, the backdrop of nesting Brown Noddies next door, and frigates overhead,

gave this place the most amazing bird charm and grace. This had to be the avian example of Pura Vida, for sure.

Mercifully, the year ended and Carol and I were on our way for another summer's tour. As it worked out, it would be our last. We headed for Kenya, and spent an equal amount of time in Tanzania. There were some new birds, but the wildebeest migration really stole the show. Even more than in South America the year prior, the grandeur of life took hold of me and wouldn't let go. It was greater than food chains and pyramids of life, greater than energy flowing through a system, greater than water and minerals being constantly recycled through a living biosphere, and frankly, it was more than a number greater than 4000 and less than 5000.

It was both disturbing and interesting to me that the closer I inched toward the neon goal, the more it was overshadowed by nature's wonders. I added the Double-toothed Barbet, but was more intrigued by each great African eagle, though none were new for me. The next lifer was a Blue Flycatcher, but the Hammercop's nest seemed much more exciting. And I even ticked off the Mariqua Sunbird, but that was overshadowed by two young male lions hanging out together, playing and making friends. What was happening to me?

We were so frustrated with Africa the second trip that we left early and flew home. After recuperating, we loaded up our Scout and spent the remaining weeks of summer in Arizona. I even added Eared Trogon to my life list, although road cruising the desert for snakes at night brought me far more enjoyment and excitement.

◀ *Brown Noddy*

I was underwhelmed to be back at school for another year, although the officers of my clubs were the best ever. It was a good year, and I found time to review the latest AOU splits and lumps. What I discovered shocked me — the Eared Trogon was actually life bird number 4998! I was only two short of the fantastic five thousand!

One of my students asked me where I would have to go to see two more life birds, and I jokingly replied "Alaska." Carol and I had since been out to Nome, as well as over many other places in the great state, and it seems I have to return there every four or five years. It just has that effect on me. So right there in my classroom, the gathering group of students decided we'd head to the Land of the Midnight Sun the following June. Five thousand, anyone?

Carol was rightfully none-too-thrilled that I had promised my students I'd take them to Alaska without talking to her about it. Our relationship was struggling because our jobs and families had us drifting apart. Frankly, I was far more motivated with my "program" than my marriage, and it was only a matter of time before that would demand the final price.

June could not come soon enough, and I bought a fifteen-passenger van to take thirteen kids to the edge of the Earth. Their luggage went in my truck, with a camper shell, driven by the male and female chaperones. More than anything else, they were invited to keep the guys and girls from co-habitating.

The kids absolutely loved the trip. We camped all the way, and the drive was considerable. I struck a deal with them that we'd only drive during daylight hours, but little did they realize that each day would be longer than the previous one, as we gained in latitude. Finally, with us roaring along in Canada at about ten at "night," one of our clever girls exclaimed that there must more daylight in the west than in the east where we'd come from. Note: I didn't teach them earth science.

It was a grand event when we finally arrived at the Alaskan border, and we played "North, to Alaska" and acted like silly tourists. The Top of the World Highway was as splendid as the first time I crested it, and my love for running tours was again felt in the strongest way. Kids hugged, gave each other high fives, and war whooped.

Soon, we were off to the North Slope, fighting the cut shale and mud. The climb up Attigan Pass that Cheryl had inspired was now a fairly tame excursion, although two or three flat tires made the trip dicey at mosquitoey times. Finally, we topped the pass, and gazed out at the Arctic Sea. The wind was howling, and snow was blowing laterally across the tundra. Down we went to the coastal tundra and every mile brought excitement to my noble band of explorers.

We camped on the tundra, and just about froze, though I do not recall anyone complaining. The next day, we walked around on the tundra, watching grizzlies, caribou, jaegers, wagtails and all sorts of neat Arctic stuff. We even had a Gyrfalcon fly right over our heads, to which Jackson and I high-fived a full foot off the ground. The kids ignored the conditions, and nature brought her storehouse to us over and over.

Finally, just below the famed pump station, I glanced at a medium-sized songbird in an Arctic Willow, just above a stream flowing near the road. It seemed odd and rather plain-colored from the back, and then it turned around. Oh, my. It was a male Bluethroat! I mumbled "oh, shoot" (that's the first fib I've told in this book) and played bird guide in a most excited way. I even waded that unbearably cold stream to get that secretive sucker out for my kids, and should have gotten pneumonia for my troubles. What I distinctly remember was stepping through that insufferably cold water and saying to myself, "I could do this." I was referring to being a bird guide.

The bird gods didn't smile on me that trip, as I remained at 4999, where the Bluethroat left me. We went to Cape Flattery in Washington, all down through California, and even the Mexican Mountains of SE Arizona (the Berylline Hummingbird vanished mere seconds before I arrived at one feeder). I was inwardly saddened that I had not fulfilled this goal, frankly, so that I could put it behind me.

It was a bittersweet trip, as I said goodbye to the best seniors I had ever known. The rising leadership didn't inspire much confidence, and it looked like a long year. I just had no idea how long.

The school administration was still mad with me for taking those kids to Alaska (like it was any of their business), and they looked for all kinds of ways to "stick it to me." Carol was mad because I hadn't called enough, and it looked like it was going to be a pretty sorry year all-around. Mostly, though, life was made so hard by loving teaching so much, and having no respect for those for whom I slaved.

That November of 1995 I moved back to Tallahassee, away from Carol, and for the first time, experienced depression that winter. I lived in the rental house I owned in Tallahassee, and hardly looked at a bird for months. When spring break mercifully came, I left for Galveston Island, where all life's pieces fell from the sky into one meaningful tapestry, and I was suddenly glimpsing my future.

What happened was that I visited the little Mecca of a forest we called Heartbreak Hammock, where I conducted graduate research years prior, and later with my students and their tents, and found it posted against trespassing. This wasn't a good start to the day, but I found the owner, and he gave me permission to bird watch there. Unbelievably, he then said they'd just decided to sell it, and at that moment, the difficulties of the year all made sense. I sat in his office (he was a contractor) and designed my soon-to-be house.

Curiously, I asked the owner why he put up the no trespassing signs after all these years, and he said that in the past, someone had been camping up there with a bunch of kids. How ironic.

Without hesitation, I called Dave Giordano, a non-lobotomized administrator in the school system, and told him I would not be returning the following year. No more dump trucks, no more disgraceful treatment of me as a teacher, no more attendance scan sheets, office personnel interrupting my class for a student who hadn't been there since day one, no more days shot by pep rallies, bomb threats, fire drills, protracted announcements, assemblies, and every other thing conceived to shortchange the learning process. Yep, as Popeye said, "That's all I can stands; I cain't stands no more!"

I returned excited and finished out the year, knowing my life was changing big-time. At the end of the summer, I loaded up most of my belongings into our famous school bus, the Enterprise, and drove it out to historic Galveston. Jackson (of Gyrfalcon fame) drove my van, and sheepishly informed me at a gas stop that the bus had been doing almost 90 mph on I-10 (the speedometer was broken). But I will never forget arriving on my property right as a spark plug blew out, driving up the hill with the subsequent sound of AK-47's firing, and scattering night-herons in all directions, with two actually hitting each other as they tried to clear the canopy.

The first month, September 1996, was tough. I spent days clearing out huge, round bollards placed there decades ago, as ranchers created a cattle pen on top for cows during hurricanes. It was dreadfully hot, but the mosquitoes were thick as thieves (in Nairobi). When I covered up, I nearly died of the heat, and when I uncovered with bug spray, the sweat took it off and they ate me alive. Worse, my new "friend" that I'm sure I would have married was killed by a drunk driver, and I felt very isolated and alone. Last, I got in trouble with Texas Parks and Wildlife for a legal bird collection I had maintained in Florida, but didn't secure permits for before moving there. All in all, that fall really sucked.

Help was on the way, though, in a most unique way. As if my former experiences weren't enough to convince me of the ornithological possibilities of this arboreal island, though, the extremely rare Connecticut Warbler showed up mid-fall, and picked my spirits up better than a full bottle of Paxil. Seven years later, my yard list stands at 281, with an amazing array of extralimital birds having wandered from Canada, Florida and The West Coast. My favorite birds, though, are the lovely eastern migrants, like Rose-breasted Grosbeaks [no.51] and Indigo Buntings [no.43], which so faithfully appear in spring, less so in fall. My favorite place is easily the "sky deck," built above the house in the heavens.

Soon, I started the Galveston Bird Club, and found a small band of birders who enjoyed being taken by van to various parks and refuges for birding. The trips were cheap, puns were free, adventure was early and often (some unsuspecting participants don't know of my penchant for racing out of the van and pouncing on snakes), and birds were never a problem. Soon there was a Mainland Bird Club, with some wonderful senior citizens from the Texas City area, and now we have added the Bolivar Birders and the Bay Area Birders. These four clubs are under the umbrella of the Nonprofit Galveston Ornithological Society, of which I am Director. Club presidents such as Richard Mayfield and Maureen Myers proved great friends, as well as the head of "Goldenwings," our traveling group, Elsie Smith [no.69].

These club presidents were with me on the ten-year mark of my father's death, on a day more complicated than most anniversaries. We were in the field with David Sibley that day, whose father is an ornithologist. And on top of that, my good friend and bird photographer extra ordinaire Brian Small was coming into Galveston as well. His ornithologist father, Dr. Arnold Small of California, passed away not long ago, certainly giving Brian and I another topic of conversation. I find myself constantly amazed what wonderful people celebrate birds (in their various ways) and what great friends they make!

It is hard to put into words how special three people have been to me professionally and personally. Two of the finest human beings I have ever known, publishers Richard and Joy Gilcrease, have become like family to me, and their generosity in promoting me professionally cannot be overstated. They have published two of my books (including Wildlife of Galveston), helped the GOS become nonprofit, and attended many of my trips. The other book, Wildlife of North Florida, basically downloaded everything I know about all Florida animals and their ecosystems, and how I wish I could have read that book when I was a budding biologist.

Equally special became Bostonian Noreen O'Brien [no.67], who moved to Galveston to become the Administrator of the GOS. Her professionalism and work ethic inspired and taught me greatly, but it was her love for birds that has left me changed forever. She would gaze at a seemingly ordinary bird out the office window and rave at its beauty. To her, the simplest birds such as wrens and sparrows (and even vireos) were incomparably lovely, and I distinctly remember poking fun at her on more than one occasion.

Not any more. Noreen is long gone to Maine after three years with us, but her insatiable desire for knowledge of birds and realization of their beauty has left its indelible mark on me forever. It is not possible for me to now contemplate even the Plain Janes of the avian world without marveling at their soft colors, sleek designs, and overall perfect color schemes (of course, I also love my nesting Painted Buntings!) [no.54].

Three more entities that live in my heart (and this will really roll your eyes) are the vehicles that brought me where I am today. My father's truck, (the Galileo) which carried my students' luggage to Alaska and back, now sits with a quarter-million miles on it, still capable of modest flight, with a plywood sign on its top, advertising my Birding Bed&Breakfast (cleverly getting around the selectively enforced sign ordinance in Galveston). The Enterprise, which liberated me from the school board, has become storage for my multitudes of junk, from camping gear to a vast array of tools. But when I slip too far away from the kids of my former life, I simply walk outside and sit in any seat, then gaze at the ceiling where hundreds of "happy campers" signed their names so many years ago. It reminds me just how real my former life was.

Even the trusty Beluga, which has carried my clients from Alaska to the Yucatan, now sits in Costa Rica (following a birding tour), a gift to a foundation trying to save the Rio Frio area. They are rebuilding it, though, and it will hardly look like the fourteenth-round fighter anymore, and will always be available for future Costa Rica trips. Like the Giving Tree, these three special cruisers will always capture my deepest sentiment, and help me to realize that "things" are not always just meaningless objects.

My favorite part of my new "job" is conducting tours for birders, from daily trips to overseas adventure. Brave souls can be assured of loads of birds, corny jokes, and usually at least one beautiful snake [no. 66].

True to my family ties in the newspaper business, I began writing bird articles for various papers soon after arriving, and now write such pieces for papers as far away as Sanibel Island, Florida. But my real joy is the nature newspaper I now publish, the Galveston Bay Gull, with articles about local birds and other animals. It is my environmental mouthpiece in a state not known as the bastion of green thought.

I also conduct environmental consultant work, teach at two local colleges, and even perform educational snake shows in local schools. Indeed, things have worked out well for me, and the heartbreak of earlier years has now turned to heartfelt happiness. Even my street name, Shaman, refers to a healer, and this troubled teacher has now been made well and reborn to birds here in paradise. But you and I both know there's one thing missing.

In 1999 — one year before the year two thousand — my life list stood one bird shy of five thousand. It had ceased to become an issue in my life, in the struggle to build my business and pay the (rather considerable) mortgage. Underneath, though, it was like an old debt, perhaps to Drs. Peterson or Stevenson, but more likely to me. I had invested a fair portion of my adult life chasing it, and don't even want to think how many thousands of dollars! It was time to put that dog to bed.

On December 5, I joined Richard, Joy and Noreen on the big bird to Venezuela, to see the avian richness of this remarkable country. We worked the Rancho Grande area, and I was able to show my three companions a bounty of new birds from fruit-eaters to antbirds, but alas, no lifers for Jim. I was truthfully just having the time of my life, but the thought of this albatross was at all times in the back of my mind.

Next was the llanos, with its clouds of waterbirds and slithering snakes. There were marvelous Hoatzins, ibis species to dazzle the best birders, monstrous Savannah and Black-collared hawks, and enough tree ducks to feed Afghanistan for a decade. Nope, no new birds here, or at the Oilbird caves of Caripe. Indeed, time was running short — at least in this millennium.

Down we went to the southeast, to the lovely (but deforested) Rio Grande. We found several neat antbirds, but none I could claim as life birds. I did reach some satisfaction by climbing a tree to snare a seven-foot snake with a frog in its mouth, only to have the freaked-out amphibian emit all kinds of gooey foam all over the snake, and subsequently, me. Following that fiasco, it was time to press on.

We worked the El Dorado area, slipping into wonderful forests recommended by my old friend, Mary Goodwin, in her great book on birding this superb country. We saw neat toucans, trogons, parrots and hummers, but nary a lifer. I loved every bird, but each was listed somewhere on my old, tattered life list. There was now only one area left.

As I promised in the journal entry quoted in chapter four, I would climb the Escalera again. More specifically, I would do it the next day, with the three most beloved people of my life. This goal was now squarely before me, and I was no longer disinterested or casual about it. Maybe quiet, but not casual. It had been long enough, and I needed closure. Tomorrow would be the day; I was sure of it.

Be sharp, look at every bird, and don't take anything for granted.

The next day was a wonderful day in the field! Each stop basically put us in a new life zone, up the Escalera toward the top of the Gran Sabana. There were more tanager species than I could shake a Cecropia limb at. I got a glimpse of a Calfbird, reveled at Paradise Tanagers, and finally heard the bong of bellbirds high atop the ancient Tepui mountain. My three wonderful friends were adding life birds faster than you could say "what's that?" That was great for them, but. . .

No life birds. Dang. We camped on the top of the first mountain that evening, and watched goatsuckers playing in the road after dark. It was truly one of the most gorgeous places on Earth, as special to me as the North Tundra. To be here with those who mean the most to me made it more special, and I temporarily forgot the burning need to wrap up the chase. It was like some cosmic Mother Nature was trying to teach me something.

The next day was one of the loveliest of my life. We drove south down the age-old, Precambrian structure, sitting quietly in awe of the majestic Tepuis far off in the distance. The flat tops reflected their indescribable age, existing even before there was life on Earth. Wondrous blackwater rivers poured from east to west across the road, spilling out into mighty waterfalls which plunged hundreds of feet down. The entire drive to Santa Elena was breathtaking, and came close to taking my mind off the goal at hand.

Two birds were possible lifers at this extreme southeastern town, but neither showed themselves. Several I had seen in the Rio de Janeiro area, two others in Guyana, and most of the balance were rather ordinary. Perhaps the best find was a Caecilian, the third class of amphibians, and virtually unknown to most Americans. Alas, it was time to quit, and head back for Caracas the next morning. All indications were that it just wasn't to be, but this was hard to accept. Even as a scientist, I found it hard to fathom my returning from Venezuela without one new bird.

We decided to make a few birding stops along the top of the Escalera, both because we never actually saw a bellbird, and also because we hadn't been here in the morning. It was the same old stuff, of course. A hummer here, a vireo there, here a swift, there a wren, everywhere a motmot. We even had our obligatory "new hummer to science" (not in the book), which translated, means we didn't see all the colors that were there, and failed to get the key field mark.

It actually wasn't long after this that we stopped at one juncture, really because it was a good parking spot. There wasn't a huge amount of activity, just a few songbirds in the treetops, and some wren testing my memory with a loud, musical song. Then it happened. All my dreams came true. The years of waiting were over. All the plane flights, the muddy walks, the miles driven through suicidal drivers, and distrustful customs agents.

I wasn't the only one to see the bird, as I glanced over and the three must-a-seers were also looking in its direction. It had fluttered into a rather barren tree, lit daintily on a lateral limb, and sat still for a moment. Oh, my word! (or something like that. . .) Looking at the profound beauty of this incredible little bird, my friends sucked in most of the free oxygen in southern Venezuela. Still, I managed to gather myself and exclaim, "It's a Scarlet-horned Manakin!"

So many things go through your mind at a time like this. My eyes teared up, as they sometimes do in excitement, and I was so out of it that I caught myself standing on my shoelaces. Briefly, I thought of the other milestone birds, such as the tiger-heron and my former students celebrating the Bluethroat that made this landmark bird possible. I thought of my dad, off in etherium somewhere, and even Carol, as a tribute for all the life birds we shared together. My heart was racing ninety to nothing, and the thin air was not coming fast enough.

It was at this exact moment that the bird had his own instruction for me. He turned sideways on the limb, bent over and erected his little scarlet horns (made of feathers, of course). He then began walking backwards on the limb, presumably courting some female, real or in his imagination. I then lost all decorum, and began imitating him along the yellow line in the road. Richard, Joy and Noreen must have though me totally insane, but I didn't care. I then held my index fingers up in the back of my head, like Kevin Costner did for the Indians when he was imitating the buffalo (it is unlikely they confused me with KC, though). Can't you just imagine this 230 pound, 6'5" man, bobbing and weaving backwards down the center line, with two little horns pointing toward the heavens?

Maybe we read too much into the insignificances that accompany huge moments, but I got a message loud and clear: Forget the number and look at the bird! Oh, I was overjoyed; I mean just crazy with excitement that my great avian journey was satisfied. But could any self-indulgent goal top the show that little bird just put on? Indeed, I find it forever poignant that the goal was exceeded by the bird itself, like Ruth and Jordan being larger than their sport. I could see all 9000 birds worldwide, and nothing could top the dancakin in the treetops.

I am so thankful for the lesson that little bird brought me on a crisp, clear morning, high atop La Gran Sabana. He removed me from the equation, and made birding about birds. Moreover, I am eternally grateful to Noreen for showing me what was really important about our feathered friends. She may struggle with the letter "R" but from her lips came the admiration for birds I should have found for myself decades ago. Lastly, I am grateful to my dad, for it is his careful practice of ornithology that I now hold as my goal in the new millennium. What can I discover about avian migration on the Upper Texas Coast, and how can it benefit the birds we all love?

Birds are so wonderful! Their colors — subtle or electric — exceed the beauty of the balance of the animal kingdom. Their songs fill the empty skies with aural companionship, from the distant chip of a Galveston phoebe in winter, to the New England wall of sound in late May. Their migration will always be the scientific personification of "miracle," as they navigate a changing Earth through the ever-changing seasons. Their eyes are the best of our planet, from the magnifying hawk vision to thrushes darting through canopies like so many Star War cruisers. Their bodies are sufficient reason to invent the word "adaptation," from their varied legs and feet to the unique wings, so specialized for the lifestyle of each species. Even the anatomy and physiology of their internal workings makes them the quintessential machine for life on this wet rock we call home. Indeed, I say carefully but confidently: There are birds, and there is the rest of the animal kingdom.

Still, what birds mean the most to me now is freedom. It is what nations fight for, and what individuals strive to find over the dump trucks and albatrosses of their lives. I have carried my burdens in my life, some within, and some without, but with each passing day, I find myself soaring on the wings of eagles more and more. And I can think of about 5000 reasons to give back to birds all that I have.

This is my new goal.

Index

INDEX